W9-ADW-400

"Susan Tassone brings the reader back to the rich mine of St. Faustina's *Diary*, this time to search for the jewels of Divine Mercy for the poor souls in purgatory. The saint's message, so beautifully presented here, is one that can and must be a part of our lives on earth as we look forward to the time when — through the grace of God — we will meet the once poor souls as joyful souls in Paradise made rich through Divine Mercy."

— Father Mitch Pacwa, S.J.

"Pope Francis has invited the Church to reflect on the corporal and spiritual works of mercy, seeing them as the standard by which we live as disciples of the Lord. An important work of mercy is to pray for the souls of those who died and are undergoing purification in purgatory. This book is a helpful resource in practicing this often-overlooked work of mercy in a more fruitful way. It is my hope that those who read it will have their hearts opened to reflect more fully on the gift of God's mercy to us and the privilege we have of sharing that mercy with others, both the living and the dead."

— Most Reverend Thomas John Paprocki
Bishop of Springfield in Illinois

"Susan Tassone's *St. Faustina Prayer Book for the Holy Souls in Purgatory* is absolutely brilliant! This passionate promoter and dear friend of the holy souls has once again put together a practical spiritual resource to aid those forgotten souls in need of prayer and sacrifices."

— MICHAEL D. WICK
Executive Director, Institute on Religious Life

"Having already written eight bestsellers on purgatory and the holy souls, now Susan Tassone — the 'Purgatory Lady' — offers yet another gem based on the moving experiences and prayers of St. Faustina, the Apostle of Mercy, in her dealings with the holy souls. Susan's latest book will inspire you to love these same holy souls, and to pray and sacrifice for them often so they may reach heaven as quickly as possible. It will also move you to live so that you may spend as little time there as possible. All you need to help the holy souls (and yourself!) can be found in these pages. Using this book, you truly can become, as Susan puts it, an 'Apostle of Purgatory.' "

— FATHER ANDREW JOSEPH APOSTOLI, CFR

"Simply put, this is a *great* book."

— FATHER DONALD H. CALLOWAY, M.I.C.

St. Faustina Prayer Book
for the Holy Souls in Purgatory

St. Faustina Prayer Book
for the Holy Souls in Purgatory

Susan Tassone

Our Sunday Visitor Publishing Division
Our Sunday Visitor, Inc.
Huntington, Indiana 46750

Nihil Obstat
Msgr. Michael Heintz, Ph.D.
Censor Librorum

Imprimatur
✠ Kevin C. Rhoades
Bishop of Fort Wayne-South Bend
November 9, 2015

The *Nihil Obstat* and *Imprimatur* are official declarations that a book is free from doctrinal or moral error. It is not implied that those who have granted the *Nihil Obstat* and *Imprimatur* agree with the contents, opinions, or statements expressed.

Our Sunday Visitor Publishing Division, Our Sunday Visitor, Inc.,
200 Noll Plaza, Huntington, IN 46750; 1-800-348-2440

ISBN: 978-1-61278-392-5 (Inventory No. 1759)
eISBN: 978-1-61278-396-3
LCCN: 2015956992

Cover design: Garrett Fosco
Cover art: Vivian Imbruglia
Interior design: Sherri L. Hoffman
Interior art: Vivian Imbruglia

PRINTED IN THE UNITED STATES OF AMERICA

To my precious friend, Lisa Mladinich,
a woman of mercy and humility,
who — like St. Faustina — sees the best in everyone
as she lovingly sacrifices for others.

Table of Contents

Editor's note: Citations at the end of quotations refer to paragraphs in the *Diary of St. Faustina Kowalska*. For example, see "(1242)" on page 25.

Personal Acknowledgments

I'm so grateful to God for putting these amazing people in my life, these friends and colleagues who helped me so much with this book.

To Bert Ghezzi, my editor at Our Sunday Visitor, whose technical expertise and ability to lay out the book was terrific. Bert, you are a man of many talents who followed through on every detail, single-handedly coordinating all the different players (near and far) who were involved in this. Your technical knowledge was most appreciated. I'm so glad you're part of the "team."

To my copy editor Bill Dodds, an award-winning novelist and wordsmith *par excellence*, who gave me award-winning ideas, and the encouragement and hope to move forward. Bill, you truly are amazing.

To Father Dan Cambra, M.I.C., whose deep devotion to St. Faustina and Divine Mercy made this book possible. Without you, Father Dan, there would be no *St. Faustina Prayer Book for the Holy Souls in Purgatory*, and I just can't thank you enough.

To Jackie Lindsey, my dear friend through nine books, my support, and the person who gives me great encouragement to keep writing. Thank you!

To Steven Jay Gross, who is beyond words and to whom I'm eternally grateful. Thank you for your unending support, friendship, wisdom, and knowledge. Steve, you're the most compassionate man I know on this earth (both to all people and animals). You're unrepeatable and irreplaceable. I would thank you from the bottom of my heart, but for you my heart is limitless.

To George Foster, a man who dots every *i* and crosses every *t*. Thank you, George, for the final editing on all my books … in your quiet, positive, professional, and faith-filled way.

To my longtime and dear friend Larry Lesof, who joined me over coffee to discuss *Rich in Mercy*. Larry, as always, you were there for me and offered wise, helpful, and excellent advice.

To Natalie Raaths, who gave me the opportunity to dig deep into St. Faustina's life. Natalie, remember to keep me in the pipeline of the books you read!

To Deacon Mike McCloskey. In 1996, long before St. Faustina was a household name, you were out front celebrating Divine Mercy Sunday. Thank you so much for introducing me to the Divine Mercy Stations, St. Faustina's favorite devotion.

To Father Anthony, Father Miguel, and Father Joseph — Franciscan Missionaries of the Eternal Word — whose love and concern for the holy souls has included promoting my books for many years. Thank you so much, dear Fathers!

To Loyola University Chicago librarians Yolande Wersching and Vanessa Crouther. Once again, your assistance was outstanding!

To Mike Wick, my "creative extraordinaire" friend, who pointed the way to a fantastic iconographer, Vivian Imbruglia, from Rancho Cucamonga, California! I'm most grateful.

To Garrett Fosco, who so generously shares his talents with others, including helping design the cover of this book. You help me "see" through an artist's eyes, and that's changed how I see the world.

To my home-team supporters, my sisters Terrie, Angel, and Claudia, a special thank you.

To Jean Studer, who is there for me. You're a wonderful, radiant woman, and I'm blessed to have you in my life.

To Fran Stortz, a powerhouse of prayer. Thank you for so faithfully keeping me, and my work, in your thoughts and prayers.

To Mary Ward, always giving and ever gracious. Thank you for traveling around the country with The Purgatory Lady.

Powerful and Personal

I have to confess I was a "Doubting Father Dan."

When I first learned this book was being considered, I thought it would be difficult — if not impossible — to make a compendium of St. Faustina's spirituality for the holy souls. Yet, here it is, in your hands.

Author Susan Tassone isn't just to be congratulated, but thanked.

I'm happy to do both.

This wonderful book not only encompasses an array of prayers, meditations, and insights from the *Diary of St. Faustina Kowalska: Divine Mercy in My Soul* but also intertwines them with beloved traditional Catholic prayers and devotions here "re-viewed" through the eyes of Divine Mercy and sharply focused on helping the holy souls in purgatory.

There is, for example, an examination of conscience based on the Corporal and Spiritual Works of Mercy, and a series of meditations from the *Diary* that can be used while praying the Rosary.

Personally, the "treasure" I was most pleased to discover was "The Seven Sorrows of Mary for the Faithful Departed." We have no knowledge of St. Faustina's familiarity with the Seven Sorrows devotion, but clearly, it fits hand-in-glove with her spirituality. And clearly — as with all the prayers in this book — it's both a powerful and personal way to help us pray for the holy souls.

That's been Susan Tassone's ministry and mission for close to two decades:

encouraging all of us to remember the Church Suffering and help speed them on their way to join the Church Triumphant.

I thank her for that, too.

— Father Dan Cambra, M.I.C.
Director of the Holy Souls Sodality

INTRODUCTION

A New Friend Named Faustina

"I have heard the Lord Jesus say that, on the Day of Judgment, He will be judging the world only in terms of mercy, because God is all Mercy. And by acting out of mercy, or neglecting mercy, a person determines their own judgment."

— St. Faustina to Sister Damiana Ziolek

Are you ready to die today? Am I?

Are we fully prepared to stand before our all-pure, all-holy God?

Even if we're in a state of grace, is it possible our snap judgment of others, selfishness, recurrent sins, pride, and long-held grudges have become such a part of our daily life that we're blind to them? Is the habit of overlooking them, dismissing them, or explaining them away so deeply engrained in us that we quickly and easily point out the speck in our neighbor's eye but fail to see the beam in our own?

Sometimes our love isn't spotless. Our ingratitude, tepid faith, lack of forgiveness, and self-centeredness hobble our relationship with God right here, right now. And on the day we die, they can stand between us and heaven.

We don't always get rid of these faults and shortcomings — these sins — during our time on earth. We may pass away with imperfections we didn't conquer ... or never tried to. And that's why the God who *is* love has given us purgatory.

That's why He offers us both the place to restore our souls and the means for that to happen.

The souls in purgatory are human beings that were weaved into the fabric of our daily lives: our families, friends, benefactors. These souls cry day and night from the depths of purgatory. They long and pine for God, their Beloved. Their tears are endless. Their suffering never ceases. They're helpless.

Pope-emeritus Benedict XVI put it this way: "[Purgatory] strips off from one person what is unbearable and from another the inability to bear certain things, so that in each of them a pure heart is revealed, and we can see that we all belong together in one enormous symphony of being" (*God and the World*, p.130).

The Catholic Church's teaching on purgatory is all about the abundance of God's mercy, love, and grace. Purgatory heals our souls of sinfulness so that we can be united with God in heaven. More than that, even now, today, God invites us to play a role in this masterpiece of His mercy. While still on earth, we can help those who are in purgatory.

Just as Jesus asked St. Faustina to cooperate in His plan of redemption — to include in her spiritual life acts of charity toward the living *and* the dead — He asks that of you. And of me.

You may be familiar with St. Faustina and the Chaplet of Divine Mercy, but what you may not know is how mercy and the needs of the souls in purgatory were intertwined throughout her life.

On the day of her final religious vows, one of St. Faustina's requests to Jesus was to free all those souls. It was that important to her, that central to her understanding of, and teaching of, God's mercy.

The purpose of this book is to share with you how we can help ourselves avoid purgatory and, at the same time, come to the aid of the suffering souls there. To show you how we can speed them home to the heavenly Father. To point out that we're on a mercy mission — with St. Faustina — to free them!

To help you become an "Apostle of Purgatory," we'll cover the seven major pillars God provides for us to relieve and release the suffering souls: doing the will of God in all things, the Mass, Scripture, the Rosary, Eucharistic Adoration, the Stations of the Cross, and the Chaplet of Divine Mercy.

Throughout this book, selected passages have been taken from the *Diary of St. Faustina Kowalska*. Those writings have had a powerful effect on me. I was overwhelmed by the love God has for us, and again reminded that we're made in His image and likeness.

On a personal level, reading St. Faustina's words has been like discovering a wonderful new friend, one who's so approachable, warm, and caring. At the same time, her *Diary* reveals that she, too, had her share of suffering. Hers was not a charmed life ... but a blessed one.

Since 1999, this is my ninth book on purgatory and the holy souls. I've given so many talks and interviews there are people who sometimes refer to me as "The Purgatory Lady." But I'll tell you something: St. Faustina has taught me even more about purgatory — and God's love and mercy — and I'm so very grateful to her for that.

She's ready to help you learn more, too. She's inviting you to join her in praying for those holy souls.

May your heart be filled with love of the holy souls in purgatory. May they walk with you in a special way all the days of your life and, in time, welcome you into paradise.

You, and the souls of your dearly departed, are in my prayers.

— SUSAN

PART I
The Essence of Divine Mercy

When I received Holy Communion, I said to Him, "Jesus, I thought about You so many times last night," and Jesus answered me, And I thought of you before I called you into being. "Jesus, in what way were You thinking about me?" In terms of admitting you to My eternal happiness. After these words, my soul was flooded with the love of God. I could not stop marveling at how much God loves us. (1292)

If I call creatures into being — that is the abyss of My mercy. (85)

The Spirituality of St. Faustina Kowalska

Today St. Maria Faustina Kowalska is known for her childlike trust in God and as His "Apostle of Mercy" because in the 1930s Our Lord asked her to proclaim His message of mercy to the whole world. And while Sister Faustina never left a series of convents and health-care facilities in pre-World War II Poland — devoting her life to sacrifice, suffering, obedience, and good works for the needy — proclaim it she did.

Following her death of multiple tuberculosis in 1938 at the age of thirty-three, her mission continued through the personal diary she had maintained to record the words of her heavenly visitors — including Jesus and Mary — and, time and again, to return to their message that at the core of God's love is His mercy.

Now Divine Mercy Sunday is celebrated worldwide on the Second Sunday of Easter. The Chaplet of Divine Mercy is prayed by countless people daily at three in the afternoon, and the Divine Mercy image of Jesus hangs in churches, chapels, and homes around the globe.

What is the message, this spirituality, that has swept through the Catholic Church and into millions of hearts over the last seven-plus decades? It's this: The essence of Divine Mercy is twofold. First, to totally trust in

Christ's mercy. And second, to show mercy to others, acting as a vessel of God's mercy.

St. Faustina wanted God's greatest attribute, His unfathomable mercy, to pass through her heart and to her neighbor. She wrote, saying to God:

[E]ach of Your saints reflects one of Your virtues; I desire to reflect Your compassionate heart, full of mercy; I want to glorify it. Let Your mercy, O Jesus, be impressed upon my heart and soul like a seal, and this will be my badge in this and the future life. Glorifying Your mercy is the exclusive task of my life. (1242)

None of this is to say that the young nun was suddenly infused with a knowledge or understanding of God's mercy. A more accurate analogy would be that God accepted her into the "School of Mercy" and there — by praying and meditating, studying Scripture and Church teaching, remaining obedient to her religious vows, suffering ever-increasing health challenges, and always being open to the promptings of the Holy Spirit — class by class, grade by grade, she grew in the wisdom and reality of God's mercy.

St. Faustina also came to know God's infinite mercy by her keen observation of Our Lady, the lives of the saints, biblical men and women, and of her daily life. In time, this included a living relationship with the angels and the souls in purgatory. In time, she came to feel and appreciate God's mercy in everything: "[W]hatever there is of good in me is Yours, O Lord" (237).

During this period, her mercy toward others deepened as she immersed herself in the Eucharist and Sacrament of Reconciliation. Jesus said to her: "[T]he strength by which you bear sufferings comes from frequent Communions. So approach this fountain of mercy often, to draw with the vessel of trust whatever you need" (1487).

We can emulate St. Faustina's tender devotion to the holy souls in our daily lives by frequenting the sacraments, developing a strong prayer life (especially the Rosary, the Way of the Cross, and the Chaplet of Divine Mercy), and visiting Our Lord in the Blessed Sacrament.

Needless to say, all this can seem daunting. Perhaps it helps to think that God has invited us to join His "School of Mercy."

Then, too, we need to remember that, as St. Faustina teaches, mercy is not found in great deeds but great love. The more we trust in Jesus, the more we'll be open to receive God's love and mercy.

A Morning Offering

[D]o what You will with me, O Jesus; I will adore You in everything. May Your will be done in me, O my Lord and my God, and I will praise Your infinite mercy. (78)

———

Today, Dear Lord, help me see others through Your eyes, through the eyes of mercy. Help me do what You ask me to do. May my words and deeds bring them comfort and hope, and may what I do — in Your name — bring souls in purgatory closer to life eternal with You. Amen.

A Prayer of Surrender to God

O Jesus, I want to live in the present moment, to live as if this were the last day of my life. I want to use every moment scrupulously for the greater glory of God, to use every circumstance for the benefit of my soul. I want to look upon everything, from the point of view that nothing happens without the will of God. God of unfathomable mercy, embrace the whole world and pour Yourself out upon us through the merciful Heart of Jesus. (1183)

———

Heavenly Father, forgive me for getting lost in worrying about the future or trapped in stewing over the past. You offer me Your mercy here and now, to be received and shared here and now. Please, Lord, help me do that. Amen.

A Litany of Mercy for the Holy Souls in Purgatory

Most merciful Jesus, You Yourself have said that You desire mercy; so I bring into the abode of Your Most Compassionate Heart the souls in Purgatory, souls who are very dear to You, and yet, who must make retribution to Your justice. May the streams of Blood and Water which gushed forth from Your Heart put out the flames of the purifying fire, that in that place, too, the power of Your mercy may be praised. (1227)

———

Eternal Father, I offer you the Body and Blood, Soul and Divinity of Your Dearly Beloved Son, Our Lord, Jesus Christ, in atonement for the sins of the souls in purgatory. Lord, have mercy.

For the sake of His sorrowful Passion, have mercy on the souls in purgatory. Christ, have mercy.

Holy God, Holy Mighty One, Holy Immortal One, have mercy on the souls in purgatory. Lord, have mercy.

For those who have died, we pray:

For members of my family,

through the mercy of God may they rest in peace.
For my friends, neighbors, and fellow parishioners …
For the priests who administered the sacraments to me …
For the religious men and women who were a part of my life …
For my teachers, counselors, and mentors …

For my schoolmates and workmates …

> *through the mercy of God may they rest in peace.*

For the doctors, nurses, and all health workers who gave me care …
For those who harmed me in any way …
For those I harmed …
For those who on earth prayed for me …
For those now in purgatory who are praying for me …
For every soul in purgatory, each one Your beloved son or daughter …

Welcome them into heaven, Dear Lord, where the perpetual light of Your mercy will shine upon them forever. Amen.

Purgatory in the Eyes of St. Faustina: Twelve Daily Meditations

Recall loved ones who have died and, in a spirit of true charity, keep in mind other departed souls who have no one on earth to pray for them. Reflect on the reality of purgatory and those who, though so close to heaven, must still prepare to enter it.

Pray for them!

Begin each day of the meditations with this prayer:

St. Faustina's Prayer for a Merciful Heart

O Jesus, I understand that Your mercy is beyond all imagining, and therefore I ask You to make my heart so big that there will be room in it for the needs of all the souls living on the face of the earth. O Jesus, my love extends beyond the world, to the souls suffering in purgatory, and I want to exercise mercy toward them by means of indulgenced prayers. God's mercy is unfathomable and inexhaustible, just as God Himself is unfathomable. Even if I were to use the strongest words there are to express this mercy of God, all this would be nothing in comparison with what it is in reality. O Jesus, make my heart sensitive to all the sufferings of my neighbor, whether of body or of soul. O my Jesus, I know that You act toward us as we act toward our neighbor.

My Jesus, make my heart like unto Your merciful Heart. Jesus, help me to go through life doing good to everyone. (692)

Day One

St. Faustina's request on the day of her perpetual vows:

Jesus, I know that today You will refuse me nothing.... Jesus, I plead with You for the souls that are most in need of prayer. I plead for the dying; be merciful to them. I also beg You, Jesus, to free all souls from purgatory. (240)

REFLECTION: Our Lord wants us to pray with zeal and fervor, to ASK BIG, to BE BOLD. We, too, can ask Our Lord to empty purgatory every day. Let us ask more than we dare. Let us be BOLD in our asking. Let us give these suffering souls to Our Lord year-round. Whom do you miss the most? Have a Mass offered for them. The Mass is the most powerful means to help the holy souls.

———

O immense Passion, O profound Wounds, O most bitter Death, O Most Precious Blood, O Sweetness above all sweetness, give them eternal rest. Amen.

Day Two

Before All Souls' Day, I went to the cemetery at dusk. Although it was locked, I managed to open the gate a bit and said, "If you need something, my dear little souls, I will be glad to help you to the extent that the rule permits me." I then heard these words, "Do the will of God; we are happy in the measure that we have fulfilled God's will." (518) I became introspective and reflected for a long time on how I am fulfilling God's will and how I am profiting from the time that God has given me. (515)

REFLECTION: There is no rebellion in purgatory. The souls there — having their wills perfectly conformed to the will of God and partaking of His goodness — remain satisfied with their condition. The holy souls live in perfect harmony with the will of God. What He wills for them is what gives them joy. At the same time, they "suffer" because they have seen God but, for a time, the Beatific Vision is taken from them. For this reason, the holy souls want us to go directly to heaven. How? Imitate St. Faustina: Do the will of God in the present moment.

———

O immense Passion, O profound Wounds, O most bitter Death, O Most Precious Blood, O Sweetness above all sweetness, give them eternal rest. Amen.

Day Three

It was at that time that I asked the Lord for whom else should I pray for. Jesus said that on the following night He would let me know for whom I should pray.

[The next night] I saw my Guardian Angel, who ordered me to follow him. In a moment I was in a misty place full of fire in which there was a great crowd of suffering souls. They were praying fervently, but to no avail, for themselves; only we can come to their aid. The flames which were burning them did not touch me at all. My Guardian Angel did not leave me for an instant. I asked these souls what their greatest suffering was. They answered me in one voice that their greatest torment was longing for God. I saw Our Lady visiting the souls in Purgatory. The souls call her "The Star of the Sea." She brings them refreshment. I wanted to talk with them some more, but my Guardian Angel beckoned me to leave. We went out of that prison of suffering. [I heard an interior voice] which said, My mercy does not want this, but justice demands it. Since that time I am in closer communion with the suffering souls. (20)

LOOK TO THE STAR

It isn't just the souls in purgatory that turn to "The Star of the Sea" but those of us still on earth, too." In the twelfth century, St. Bernard of Clairvaux wrote:

If the winds of temptation arise;
If you are driven upon the rocks of tribulation look to the star, call on Mary;
If you are tossed upon the waves of pride, of ambition, of envy, of rivalry, look to the star, call on Mary.
Should anger, or avarice, or fleshly desire violently assail the frail vessel of your soul, look at the star, call upon Mary.

REFLECTION: The angels are active in purgatory consoling the holy souls, and inspiring friends and relatives to offer a Mass and practice good deeds for their dearly departed. The angels tell those in purgatory who, on earth, is praying for them. Later, they escort the souls to heaven with the speed of lightning. Have a great devotion to your guardian angels. Ask their help to purify your soul here on earth. Their charge is to get you home to heaven. They are intent obtaining all the graces and favors from God for your eternal welfare.

The Blessed Virgin fulfills her role as Mediatrix of Mercy. God distributes His mercies through her. She exercises her maternal role to the holy souls in purgatory by bringing them refreshment and hastening their release. Entrust your life to Mary, the most holy Star of the Sea, so she may lead you to Jesus.

―――

O immense Passion, O profound Wounds, O most bitter Death, O Most Precious Blood, O Sweetness above all sweetness, give them eternal rest. Amen.

Day Four

On April 29, 1926, the soul of Sister Henry, who had recently died, asked St. Faustina to have one Mass offered for her and say the Eternal Rest Prayer three times for her. After St. Faustina had done that, Sister Henry's soul returned and said with gratitude, "May God repay you" (21).

REFLECTION: Devotion to the holy souls in purgatory isn't some sort of "extra" Christian charity. (We certainly wouldn't feel that way if we were in our neighbor's place there!) Not just a responsibility, it's a God-given honor and a privilege for all of us, young and old alike. And our Heavenly Father, who sees what we're doing to help the souls, will reward us with more graces and blessings than we can even imagine. No one can outdo the generosity of God.

O immense Passion, O profound Wounds, O most bitter Death, O Most Precious Blood, O Sweetness above all sweetness, give them eternal rest. Amen.

Day Five

After Vespers today, there was a procession to the cemetery. I could not go, because I was on duty at the gate. But that did not stop me at all from praying for the souls. As the procession was returning from the cemetery to the chapel, my soul felt the presence of many souls. I understood the great justice of God, how each one had to pay off the debt to the last cent. (1375) Most Merciful Heart of Jesus, protect us from the just anger of God. (1526) O Jesus, shield me with Your mercy and also judge me leniently, or else Your justice may rightly damn me. (1093)

REFLECTION: It is God's burning love, His longing for the holy souls, that creates their longing for Him. They burn for love of Him. Hearts flame for love of Him. They have an unquenchable thirst, an unspeakable yearning for Him, a "heartsickness" for Him. This is the essence of purgatory.

O immense Passion, O profound Wounds, O most bitter Death, O Most Precious Blood, O Sweetness above all sweetness, give them eternal rest. Amen.

Day Six

One evening, one of the deceased sisters, who had already visited me a few times, appeared to me. The first time I had seen her, she had been in great suffering, and then gradually these sufferings had diminished; this time she was radiant with happiness, and she told me she was already in heaven.... And further as a sign that she only now was in heaven, God would bless our house. Then she came closer to me, embraced me sincerely and said, "I must go now." I understood how closely the three stages of a soul's life are bound together; that is to say, life on earth, in purgatory and in heaven [the Communion of Saints]. (594)

"... God loves in a special way those whom we love." (1438)

[H]ow very easy it is to become holy; all that is needed is a bit of good will. If Jesus sees this little bit of good will in the soul, He hurries to give Himself to the soul, and nothing can stop Him, neither shortcomings nor falls — absolutely nothing. (291) May you be blessed, O God, for everything You send me. Nothing under the sun happens without Your will. (1208)

REFLECTION: The holy souls in purgatory can no longer sin. They can no longer offend God. They want us to become saints. The saints experienced stress, temptations, and struggles. However, the saints became holy with these crosses. Choosing God is how we become holy. Prayer redirects our will. Aligning our life with the will of God will lead us directly to heaven.

———

O immense Passion, O profound Wounds, O most bitter Death, O Most Precious Blood, O Sweetness above all sweetness, give them eternal rest. Amen.

Day Seven

One night, a sister who had died two months previously came to me.... I saw her in a terrible condition.... A shudder went through my soul because I did not know whether she was suffering in purgatory or in hell. Nevertheless, I redoubled my prayers for her. The next night she came again, but I saw her in an even more horrible state … and despair was written all over her face. I was astonished to see her in a worse condition after the prayers I had offered for her, and I asked, "Haven't my prayers helped you?" She answered that my prayers had not helped her and that nothing would help her. I said to her, "And the prayers which the whole community has offered for you, have they not been any help to you?" She said no, that these prayers had helped some other souls. I replied, "If my prayers are not helping you, Sister, please stop coming to me." She disappeared at once. Despite this, I kept on praying.

After some time she came back again to me during the night, but already her appearance had changed … her face was radiant, her eyes beaming with joy. She told me I had a true love for my neighbor and that many other souls had profited from my prayers. She urged me not to cease praying for the souls in purgatory, and she added that she herself would not remain there much longer. How astounding are the decrees of God! (58)

REFLECTION: We need the urgings of the holy souls, and we need grace. When we show compassion to them, the holy souls with their powerful influence will never fail us. Above all, they come to your aid in the salvation of your soul and relief in the agonies of death before God's judgment seat. Double up on your acts of charity for the suffering souls. What we give comes back beyond belief. Become their deliverers and they will become your powerful intercessors forever.

—

O immense Passion, O profound Wounds, O most bitter Death, O Most Precious Blood, O Sweetness above all sweetness, give them eternal rest. Amen.

Day Eight

The mercy of the Lord is praised by the holy souls in heaven who have themselves experienced that infinite mercy. What these souls do in heaven, I already will begin to do here on earth. I will praise God for His infinite goodness, and I will strive to bring other souls to know and glorify the inexpressible and incomprehensible mercy of God. (753)

REFLECTION: Purgatory is not just doctrinal, it's also pastoral because it provides hope and healing. All that is part of the Gospel and that's good news. Pass it on!

———

O immense Passion, O profound Wounds, O most bitter Death, O Most Precious Blood, O Sweetness above all sweetness, give them eternal rest. Amen.

Day Nine

July 9, 1937. This evening, one of the deceased sisters came and asked me for one day of fasting and to offer all my [spiritual] exercises on that day for her. I answered that I would. (1185) From early morning on the following day, I offered everything for her intention. During Holy Mass, I had a brief experience of her torment. I experienced such intense hunger for God that I seemed to be dying of the desire to become united with Him. This lasted only a short time, but I understood what the longing of the souls in purgatory was like. (1186) This day, my spirit was set aflame with special love for the Eucharist. It seemed to me that I was transformed into a blazing fire. (160)

REFLECTION: Even before St. Faustina entered the community, she acquired from her employers the right to attend Mass, go to confession, and visit the sick and dying. Her austere lifestyle included exhaustive fasting.

To appease God's anger and obtain His mercy for the sins committed against the Lord, Moses observed a fast for forty days and nights. We're invited to follow Moses and fast and pray for the relief of the suffering souls. Fasting shows solidarity with them. They're not alone or forgotten. Fasting also persuades others to help them. Fasting creates a link between the living and the dead. To release the holy souls from the anguish of purgatory, fast for them. This is a perfect act of love to end their anguish. Fasting is a key to God's heart and mercy!

—

O immense Passion, O profound Wounds, O most bitter Death, O Most Precious Blood, O Sweetness above all sweetness, give them eternal rest. Amen.

CATHOLIC TEACHING ON FASTING

"The Gospels speak of a time of solitude for Jesus in the desert immediately after his baptism by John. Driven by the Spirit into the desert, Jesus remains there for forty days without eating" (*Catechism of the Catholic Church* [CCC] 538).

"By the solemn forty days of *Lent* the Church unites herself each year to the mystery of Jesus in the desert" (CCC 540).

"The interior penance of the Christian can be expressed in many and various ways. Scripture and the Fathers insist above all on three forms, *fasting, prayer, and almsgiving,* which express conversion in relation to oneself, to God, and to others" (CCC 1434).

"The fourth precept [of the Church] ('You shall observe the days of fasting and abstinence established by the Church') ensures the times of ascesis [self-discipline] and penance which prepare us for the liturgical feasts and help us acquire mastery over our instincts and freedom of heart" (CCC 2043).

Day Ten

When I had gone to the chapel for a moment, the Lord gave me to know that, among His chosen ones, there are some who are especially chosen, and whom He calls to a higher form of holiness, to exceptional union with Him. These are seraphic souls, from whom God demands greater love than He does from others.... Such a soul understands this call because God makes this known to it interiorly, but the soul may either follow this call or not.... I have learned that there is a place in purgatory where souls will pay their debt to God for such transgressions; this kind of torment is the most difficult of all. The soul which is specially marked by God will be distinguished everywhere, whether in heaven or in purgatory or in hell. In heaven, it will be distinguished from other souls by greater glory and radiance and deeper knowledge of God. In purgatory, by greater pain, because it knows God more profoundly and desires Him more vehemently. In hell, it will suffer more profoundly than other souls, because it knows more fully whom it has lost. This indelible mark of God's exclusive love, in the [soul], will not be obliterated. (1556)

REFLECTION: The religious and clergy have more means of meriting and expiating their daily faults during life. The most abandoned souls are clergy and consecrated religious. We tend to canonize our religious and leave off too soon our prayers for them. God bestowed special graces to these souls. A more faithful cooperation was demanded. Our prayers are critical for these chosen souls.

———

O immense Passion, O profound Wounds, O most bitter Death, O Most Precious Blood, O Sweetness above all sweetness, give them eternal rest. Amen.

Day Eleven

I sometimes talk too much. A thing could be settled in one or two words, and as for me, I take too much time about it. But Jesus wants me to use that time to say some short indulgenced prayers for the souls in purgatory. And the Lord says that every word will be weighed on the day of judgment. (274)

Oh, how good it is to call on Jesus for help during a conversation. Oh, how good it is, during a moment of peace, to beg for actual graces.... [T]here is need of much divine light at times like this, in order to speak with profit, both for the other person's soul, and for one's own as well. God, however, comes to our aid; but we have to ask Him for it. Let no one trust too much in his own self. (1495)

There is life, but there is also death in the tongue. Sometimes we kill with the tongue: we commit real murders. And we are still to regard that as a small thing?... O my silent Jesus, have mercy on us! (119)

REFLECTION: *Jesus said this to St. Faustina about a talkative soul:* "I find no rest in such a soul. The constant din tires Me, and in the midst of it the soul cannot discern My voice" (1008). *Take time to keep silent throughout the day.*

———

O immense Passion, O profound Wounds, O most bitter Death, O Most Precious Blood, O Sweetness above all sweetness, give them eternal rest. Amen.

Day Twelve

Once I was summoned to the judgment [seat] of God. I stood alone before the Lord. Jesus appeared such as we know Him during His Passion. After a moment, His wounds disappeared except for five, those in His hands, His feet and His side. Suddenly I saw the complete condition of my soul as God sees it. I could clearly see all that is displeasing to God. I did not know that even the smallest transgressions will have to be accounted for. What a moment! Who can describe it? To stand before the Thrice-Holy God! (36)

REFLECTION: Blessed Michael Sopocko, spiritual director of St. Faustina, echoes:

> The souls in purgatory are certain of their salvation, know the state of their soul, are confirmed in good, and love the merciful God. All this affords them great relief in their suffering. Their knowledge of the infinite holiness of God and of their own unworthiness to behold God is great, and prompts them to bear their sufferings willingly and with utter abandonment to the will of God, since these sufferings are the means of their purification and satisfaction for their sins. Moved by contrition the souls in purgatory would rather not go to heaven than stand before God without their wedding garments. They cannot help themselves, and their only relief is God's mercy which awakens the Christians on earth to make sacrifices for them. (*God Is Mercy*, pp. 90-91)

O immense Passion, O profound Wounds, O most bitter Death, O Most Precious Blood, O Sweetness above all sweetness, give them eternal rest. Amen.

An Examination of Conscience Based on the Corporal and Spiritual Works of Mercy

Jesus told St. Faustina:

> [W]rite this for the many souls who are often worried because they do not have the material means with which to carry out an act of mercy. Yet spiritual mercy, which requires neither permissions nor

storehouses, is much more meritorious and is within the grasp of every soul. If a soul does not exercise mercy somehow or other, it will not obtain My mercy on the day of judgment. Oh, if only souls knew how to gather eternal treasure for themselves, they would not be judged, for they would forestall My judgment with their mercy. (1317)

The spirituality of St. Faustina's order, the Congregation of Sisters of Our Lady of Mercy, included the apostolate of the corporal and spiritual works of mercy. Each of those works can be a way for us to assist the suffering souls.

Unite the Corporal and Spiritual works of Mercy with the Merciful Christ for the Suffering Souls. Let us bring comfort to the destitute and healing to those who suffer in body or spirit. Living out these works of mercy can be the direct means into heaven — the hunger, the thirst, the famine, and the drought for God is the prayer of purgatory. These holy heroes are in desperate need of our good works and sacrifices.

May God's grace manifest itself in our efforts for the living and for the sake of the deceased. Who do you wish you could have done more for? Strive to perform one act of mercy each day in his or her honor.

St. Faustina tells us: "Let us beware of adding to the suffering of others, because that is displeasing to the Lord" (117).

The Corporal Works of Mercy

Feed the hungry.

Do I contribute (money, food, or volunteer hours) to my local food bank or the St. Vincent de Paul conference in my parish? Do I take a friend or family member who's having financial difficulties out to lunch or dinner? Do I notice and positively respond to someone at work, in the neighborhood, or at the parish who "hungers" for a kind word, a bit of recognition for a job well done, or someone to listen — if only for a few minutes — to the challenges he or she is facing? Do I remember the hungry in my prayers? At the Final Judgment, will Jesus say to me: "I was hungry and you gave me no food" (Mt 25:42)? What does Divine Mercy ask me, invite me, to do today?

Give drink to the thirsty.

Do I thank God that clean drinking water is cheap and plentiful in my home? Do I express that gratitude by helping make that possible in other countries? Is there someone I know who "thirsts" for my friendship or my forgiveness? Do I remember the thirsty in my prayers? At the Final Judgment, will Jesus say to me: "I was thirsty and you gave me no drink" (Mt 25:42)? What does Divine Mercy ask me, invite me, to do today?

Clothe the naked.

Am I quick to complain that I've run out of closet space but refuse to donate items I no longer need or wear? Am I spending money on new clothes just to be "in style" when others in my community are trying to get by with clothes that are no longer usable at all? Have I looked into how part of my "clothing budget" can be given to organizations that help clothe those in need? Am I so wrapped up in myself that I don't even see those around me who are hurting, or who *I'm* hurting. Do I remember those in need of clothing in my prayers? At the Last Judgment, will Jesus say to me: "I was … naked and you did not clothe me" (Mt 25:43)? What does Divine Mercy ask me, invite me, to do today?

Shelter the homeless.

Am I critical of those who live on the streets or can't pay their rents or have defaulted on their mortgages? Do I donate to organizations that assist them? Do I refuse to give even a dollar to someone begging on the street because "I know he'll only use it for drugs or alcohol"? Is there someone I know who's "homeless" because he or she has no family or friends? Do I, for a holiday meal or other occasion, say "my home is your home"? Do I remember the homeless in my prayers? What does Divine Mercy ask me, invite me, to do today?

Visit the sick.

Do I make the effort to send a note or e-mail, make a call, or pay a visit to someone who is sick? Have I considered becoming an extraordinary minister of the Eucharist to bring Christ to the homebound and those in nursing homes or hospitals? Do I offer to assist a family member who's taking care of a sick loved one? Could I drive a frail or elderly neighbor or parishioner to a doctor's appointment? Have I ever acknowledged and thanked a family caregiver for what he or she is doing? Do I remember care-receivers and caregivers in my prayers? At the Final Judgment, will Jesus say to me, "I was … sick … and you did not visit me" (Mt 25:43)? What does Divine Mercy ask me, invite me, to do today?

Visit the imprisoned.

Do I limit my mercy only to those who are "wrongfully" imprisoned? Has it ever occurred to me that, after His arrest, Jesus was a prisoner? Have I looked into what I can do to help those who are incarcerated and help their loved ones? Have I donated to the organizations that help both of those populations? Do I remember the imprisoned and their loved ones in my prayers? At the Final Judgment, will Jesus say to me: "I was … in prison and you did not visit me" (Mt 25:43)? What does Divine Mercy ask me, invite me, to do today?

Bury the dead.

Do I avoid attending the funeral of a family member, friend, or colleague because I don't like to think about death or because going inconveniences me? Do I have a Mass said for his or her soul? Do I send the grieving family flowers or a card? Do I bring food to their house or have it sent to them? If appropriate, do I help with the funeral or burial expenses? Do I volunteer at the parish to supply a dish for the funeral reception or help serve the meal? What does Divine Mercy ask me, invite me, to do today?

The Spiritual Works of Mercy

Admonish the sinner.

Do I take this work of mercy as a personal license to judge others and their actions? On the other hand, do I hesitate to speak or act because the thought of that makes me uncomfortable, or do I think, "That's not my responsibility"? Would it be better if I substituted the words "gently correct" for "admonish"? At the very least, do I pray for those who are steeped in sin? What does Divine Mercy ask me, invite me, to do today?

Instruct the ignorant.

Do I take an unhealthy pride in my knowing about God and His love, as if the gift of faith was something I earned? As if my knowledge of His ways was something I figured out on my own? How do I use that faith, that knowledge, to help others learn of Him and his love for them? Do I follow the advice often attributed to St. Francis of Assisi: "Preach the Gospel always. If necessary, use words"? Who, by my actions and example, can learn more about our Heavenly Father? What does Divine Mercy ask me, invite me, to do today?

Counsel the doubtful.

Am I quick to overwhelm, bully, shame, or attempt to "out debate" those who have questions about God or the Church? Am I afraid to prayerfully consider my own doubts and spend the time and make the effort to seek the answers the Holy Spirit is waiting to give me? Do I give others the impression that I'm so sure and certain all the time that my faith doesn't include accepting mysteries that are beyond my ability of understanding? What does Divine Mercy ask me, invite me, to do today?

Comfort the afflicted.

Do I avoid those who are grieving the loss of a loved one because "I don't know what to say, and I don't want to say the wrong thing." Do I let my discomfort of being around those overwhelmed with sorrow keep me from doing *anything* to help them? Do I assume grief is over in a short amount of time, that one reaches "closure" and then all is well for that person? Do I break ties with someone who grieves the death of a loved one because I don't like thinking about death? When was the last time I prayed for someone who is grieving? Someone who has lost his or her job or home? Someone whose life has been turned upside down? What does Divine Mercy ask me, invite me, to do today?

Bear wrongs patiently.

Do I get angry at God, others, and the world when — it seems to me — life isn't fair! At those times, do I even consider the heartaches and hardships that were a part of the lives of Jesus and Mary? Do I ask God to give me more patience and then quickly add "Now!"? Do I take advantage of the times I am wronged by offering them up as a prayer for the souls in purgatory and for those on earth most in need of prayers? What does Divine Mercy ask me, invite me, to do today?

Forgive all injuries.

Do I hate to give up long-held grudges because, in some way, they give me comfort? Am I unwilling to offer unconditional forgiveness? ("I'll forgive you but only if you admit…." or "I'm not the one who has to make the first move.") Do I wish ill on those who have hurt me and take pleasure when that happens? Do I say the Our Father — "forgive us our trespasses, as we forgive those who trespass against us" — with a hasty "yes but …" mentally inserted in it? Do I ever consider how my lack of forgiving is hampering my relationship with God? Have I asked God to help me forgive? What does Divine Mercy ask me, invite me, to do today?

Pray for the living and the dead.

Do I frequently pray for my wants before I pray for the needs of others? Am I quick to tell someone who could use some prayers that I will pray for him or her … and then do it? Do I have Masses said for my loved ones still on earth, and Masses and Gregorian Masses for the souls of those who have died? Do I take advantage of the fact that offering up hardships, fasting, and making donations to worthy causes are another form of "praying" for others? Do I humbly ask others — especially the elderly and the very young — to pray for me and promise to keep them in my prayers? What does Divine Mercy ask me, invite me, to do today?

Act of Contrition

O my God, I am heartily sorry for having offended You, and I detest all of my sins because of Your just punishments, but most of all because I have offended You, my God, who are all good and deserving of all my love. I firmly resolve, with the help of Your grace, to sin no more and to avoid the near occasions of sin. Amen.

[Our Lord to St. Faustina:] Call upon My mercy on behalf of sinners; I desire their salvation. When you say this prayer, with a contrite heart and with faith on behalf of some sinner, I will give him the grace of conversion. This is the prayer:

"O Blood and Water, which gushed forth from the Heart of Jesus as a fount of Mercy for us, I trust in You." (186-187)

A Prayer of Trust in Infinite Mercy

O God, show me Your mercy
According to the compassion of the Heart of Jesus.
Hear my sighs and entreaties,
And the tears of a contrite heart.

O Omnipotent, ever-merciful God,
Your compassion is never exhausted.
Although my misery is as vast as the sea,
I have complete trust in the mercy of the Lord.

O Eternal Trinity, yet ever-gracious God,
Your compassion is without measure.
And so I trust in the sea of Your mercy,
And sense You, Lord, though a veil holds me aloof.

May the omnipotence of Your mercy, O Lord,
Be glorified all over the world.
May its veneration never cease.
Proclaim, my soul, God's mercy with fervor. (1298)

PART II
Praying in the Presence of Our Lord with St. Faustina

Eucharistic Adoration and the Holy Souls

Eucharistic Adoration is one of the most powerful forms of prayer in assisting the holy souls to reach God. Nothing gives God more glory, or brings Him greater joy, than when we remember those who have died. And there is no better way to pray for the holy souls in purgatory than during Eucharistic Adoration. Intercession at Adoration speeds them home to heaven.

The adorers assume the office of mediators on behalf of the holy souls. By their unceasing prayers, they offer up supplications day and night to the throne of God's mercy on behalf of the Church Suffering. Our intercessory prayers give the suffering souls great comfort. From the Sacred Host, streams of alleviating grace flow into the expiatory realms of purgatory, bringing unspeakable relief to those imprisoned there.

The spirituality of St. Faustina and her congregation had a strong Eucharistic element, including making Eucharistic Holy Hours in reparation for the sins of the world. Sister Maria Faustina of the Most Blessed Sacrament was St. Faustina's full religious name. She chose it because she had great love and devotion to the Holy Eucharist. She said: "The courage and strength that are in me are not of me, but of Him who lives in me — it is the Eucharist. O my Jesus, the misunderstandings are so great; sometimes, were it not for the Eucharist, I would not have the courage to go any further along the way You have marked out for me" (91).

She also wrote: "I spend every moment at the feet of the hidden God.... Here I obtain strength and light; here I learn everything; here I am given light on how to act toward my neighbor" (704).

Prayers of St. Faustina Before the Eucharist

When, during adoration, I repeated the prayer, "Holy God" several times, a vivid presence of God suddenly swept over me, and I was caught up in spirit before the majesty of God. I saw how the Angels and the Saints of the Lord give glory to God. The glory of God is so great that I dare not try to describe it, because I would not be able to do so, and souls might think that what I have written is all there is. (1604)

Bread of Angels

I bow down before You, O Bread of Angels,
With deep faith, hope, and love.
And from the depths of my soul I worship You,
Though I am but nothingness.

I bow down before You, O hidden God,
And love You with all my heart.
The veils of mystery hinder me not at all;
I love You as do Your chosen ones in heaven.

I bow down before You, O Lamb of God
Who take away the sins of my soul,
Whom I receive into my heart each morn,
You who are my saving help. (1324)

Divine Prisoner of Love

O Jesus, Divine Prisoner of Love, when I consider Your love and how you emptied Yourself for me, my senses fail me. You hide Your inconceivable majesty and lower Yourself to miserable me. O King of Glory, though You hide Your beauty, yet the eye of my soul rends the veil. I see the angelic choirs giving You honor without cease, and all the heavenly Powers praising You without cease, and without cease they are saying: Holy, Holy, Holy ... with chanting so delightful that no human tongue could ever match it. (80, 1111)

Prayer in Praise of the Blessed Host

O Living Host, my one and only strength, fountain of love and mercy, embrace the whole world.... Oh, blessed be the instant and the moment when Jesus left us His most merciful Heart! (223)

O Blessed Host, in whom is contained the testament of God's mercy for us, and especially for poor sinners.

O Blessed Host, in whom is contained the Body and Blood of the Lord Jesus as proof of infinite mercy for us, and especially poor sinners.

O Blessed Host, in whom contained life eternal and of infinite mercy, dispensed in abundance to us and especially to poor sinners.

O Blessed Host, in whom is contained the mercy of the Father, the Son, and the Holy Spirit toward us, and especially toward poor sinners.

O Blessed Host, in whom is contained the infinite price of mercy which will compensate for all our debts, and especially those of poor sinners.

O Blessed Host, in whom is contained the fountain of living water which springs from infinite mercy for us, and especially for poor sinners.

O Blessed Host, in whom is contained the fire of purest love which blazes forth from the bosom of the Eternal Father, as from an abyss of infinite mercy for us, and especially for poor sinners.

O Blessed Host, in whom is contained the medicine for our infirmities, flowing from infinite mercy, as from a fount, for us and especially for poor sinners.

O Blessed Host, in whom is contained the union between God and us through His infinite mercy for us, and especially for poor sinners.

O Blessed Host, in whom are contained all the sentiments of the most sweet Heart of Jesus toward us, and especially poor sinners.

O Blessed Host, our only hope in all the sufferings and adversities of life.

O Blessed Host, our only hope in the midst of darkness and of storms within and without.

O Blessed Host, our only hope in life and at the hour of our death.

O Blessed Host, our only hope in the midst of adversities and floods of despair.

O Blessed Host, our only hope in the midst of falsehood and treason.

O Blessed Host, our only hope in the midst of the darkness and godlessness which inundate the earth.

O Blessed Host, our only hope in the longing and pain in which no one will understand us.

O Blessed Host, our only hope in the toil and monotony of everyday life.

O Blessed Host, our only hope amid the ruin of our hopes and endeavors.

O Blessed Host, our only hope in the midst of the ravages of the enemy and the efforts of hell.

O Blessed Host, I trust in You when the burdens are beyond my strength and I find my efforts are fruitless.

O Blessed Host, I trust in You when storms toss my heart about and my fearful spirit tends to despair.

O Blessed Host, I trust in You when my heart is about to tremble and mortal sweat moistens my brow.

O Blessed Host, I trust in You when everything conspires against me and black despair creeps into my soul.

O Blessed Host, I trust in You when my eyes will begin to grow dim to all temporal things and, for the first time, my spirit will behold the unknown worlds.

O Blessed Host, I trust in You when my tasks will be beyond my strength and adversity will become my daily lot.

O Blessed Host I trust in You when the practice of virtue will appear difficult for me and my nature will grow rebellious.

O Blessed Host, I trust in You when hostile blows will be aimed against me.

O Blessed Host, I trust in You when my toils and efforts will be misjudged by others.

O Blessed Host, I trust in You when Your judgments will resound over me; it is then that I will trust in the sea of Your mercy. (356)

"Eternal Father, I offer you the Most Precious Blood of Thy Divine Son, Jesus, in union with the Masses said throughout the world today, for all the holy souls in purgatory, for sinners everywhere, those in the Universal Church, in my home and in my own family. Amen."

— EUCHARISTIC PRAYER OF ST. GERTRUDE

O Holy Trinity, One and Indivisible God, may You be blessed for the great gift and testament of mercy. (81)

I Adore You, Lord

I adore You, Lord and Creator, hidden in the Blessed Sacrament. I adore You for all the works of Your hands, that reveal to me so much wisdom, goodness and mercy, O Lord. You have spread so much beauty over the earth and it tells me about Your beauty, even though these beautiful things are but a faint reflection of You, Incomprehensible Beauty. And although You have hidden Yourself and concealed Your beauty, my eye, enlightened by faith, reaches You, and my soul recognizes its Creator, its Highest Good; and my heart is completely immersed in prayer of adoration. (1692)

Your Goodness Encourages Me

My Lord and Creator, Your goodness encourages me to converse with You. Your mercy abolishes the chasm which separates the Creator from the creature. To converse with You, O Lord, is the delight of my heart. In You I find everything that my heart could desire. Here Your light illumines my mind, enabling it to know You more and more deeply. Here streams of graces flow down upon my heart. Here my soul draws eternal life. O my Lord and Creator, You alone, beyond all these gifts, give Your own self to me and unite Yourself intimately with Your miserable creature. (1692)

In Praise of Infinite Mercy

O Christ, I am most delighted when I see that You are loved, and that Your praise and glory resound, especially the praise of Your Mercy. O Christ, to the last moment of my life, I will not stop glorifying Your goodness and mercy. With every drop of my blood, with every beat of my heart, I glorify Your mercy. I long to be entirely transformed into a hymn of Your glory. When I find myself on my deathbed, may the last beat of my heart be a loving hymn in praise of Your unfathomable mercy. (1708)

Spiritual Communion

Spiritual Communion consists of an ardent desire to receive Jesus in the Most Holy Sacrament and lovingly embracing Him as if we had actually received Him.

———

My Jesus, I believe that You are truly present in the Most Blessed Sacrament. I love You above all things, and I desire to possess You within my soul. Since I am unable now to receive You sacramentally, come at least spiritually into my heart. I embrace You as being already there, and unite myself wholly to You. Never permit me to be separated from You. Amen.

The Sacred Heart and Divine Mercy

During his 2001 homily at the first universally celebrated Divine Mercy Sunday, St. John Paul II said:

> Let us relive this moment with great spiritual intensity. Today the Lord also shows us His glorious wounds and His Heart, an inexhaustible source of light and truth, of love and forgiveness....
>
> His "Sacred Heart" has given men everything: redemption, salvation, sanctification. St. Faustina Kowalska saw coming from this Heart that was overflowing with generous love two rays of light which illuminated the world. "The two rays," according to what Jesus himself told her, "represent the blood and the water" (*Diary*, p. 132). The blood recalls the sacrifice of Golgotha and the mystery of the Eucharist; the water, according to the rich symbolism of the

Evangelist John, makes us think of Baptism and the Gift of the Holy Spirit (cf. Jn 3:5; 4:14).

Jesus said to St. Faustina: "These rays of mercy will pass through you, just as they have passed through this Host, and they will go out through all the world" (441).

Through the mystery of this wounded Heart, the restorative tide of God's merciful love continues to spread over the men and women of our time. Here alone can those who long for true and lasting happiness find its secret. Offer your Holy Hour for your deceased relatives and friends, priests and consecrated religious, the most abandoned souls in purgatory. Fix your gaze on Jesus.

St. Faustina and the Attributes of God

The holy souls are cleansed by the attributes of God. In heaven, God's attributes — His glory, power, sanctity, truth, wisdom, and beatitude — will be shared with us in greater measure than any of God's gifts on earth. This is the work of purgatory. Marvelous is the mercy of God to have provided sinners with a purgatory that finishes the lifework that the neglectful soul has left undone.

> During Advent, a great yearning for God arose in my soul. My spirit rushed toward God with all its might. During that time, the Lord gave me much light to know His attributes.
>
> The first attribute which the Lord gave me to know is His holiness. His holiness is so great that all the Powers and Virtues tremble before Him. The pure spirits veil their faces and lose themselves in unending adoration, and with one single word they express the highest form of adoration; that is — Holy.... The holiness of God is poured out upon

the Church of God and upon every living soul in it, but not in the same degree. There are souls who are completely penetrated by God, and there are those who are barely alive.

The second kind of knowledge which the Lord granted me concerns His justice. His justice is so great and penetrating that it reaches deep into the heart of things, and all things stand before Him in naked truth, and nothing can withstand Him.

The third attribute is love and mercy. And I understood that the greatest attribute is love and mercy. It unites the creature with the Creator. This immense love and abyss of mercy are made known in the Incarnation of the Word and in the Redemption [of humanity], and it is here that I saw this as the greatest of all God's attributes. (180)

St. Faustina's Prayer for Priests

Priests and consecrated religious are some of the most abandoned souls. We are apt to quickly stop our praying for them because we assume they're freed from purgatory sooner than they are.

During our Holy Hour before the Blessed Sacrament, let's include prayers for those consecrated to God. We'll gain fresh intercessors who will pray for us now, and who will surround us at the hour of our death.

December 17, [1936]. I have offered this day for priests. I have suffered more today than ever before, both interiorly and exteriorly. I did not know it was possible to suffer so much in one day. I tried to make a Holy Hour, in the course of which my spirit had a taste of the bitterness of the Garden of Gethsemane. I am fighting alone, supported by His arm, against all the difficulties that face me like unassailable walls. But I trust in the power of His name and I fear nothing. (823)

Grant Love and Light to Our Priests

O my Jesus, I beg You on behalf of the whole Church: Grant it love and the light of Your Spirit, and give power to the words of priests so that hardened hearts might be brought to repentance and return to You, O Lord. Lord, give us holy priests; You yourself maintain them in holiness. O Divine and Great High Priest, may the power of Your mercy accompany them everywhere and protect them from the devil's traps and snares which are continually being set for the souls of priests. May the power of Your mercy, O Lord, shatter and bring to naught all that might tarnish the sanctity of priests, for You can do all things. (1052)

An Offering in Reparation for the Holy Souls

My Jesus, support me when difficult and stormy days come, days of testing, days of ordeal, when suffering and fatigue begin to oppress my body and my soul. Sustain me, Jesus, and give me strength to bear suffering. Set a guard upon my lips that they may address no word of complaint to creatures. Your most merciful Heart is all my hope. I have nothing for my defense but only Your mercy; in it lies all my trust. (1065)

Acts of Faith, Hope, and Charity for the Holy Souls

As St. Louis Guanella wrote, "The holy souls in purgatory will obtain for us an increase of the virtues of faith, hope, and charity. Faith will open the doors of paradise and will kindle in us the light of joy that radiates heaven. Hope will lift us away from the mire of the earth and will lead us by the hand to ascent up high. Charity will say 'Come, Come!' and give us strength and carry us in its bosom until we are in the presence of the Most High God." Pray these acts of virtues frequently.

Acts of Faith

I want to live in the spirit of faith. I accept everything that comes my way as given me by the loving will of God, who sincerely desires my happiness. And so I will accept with submission and gratitude everything that God sends me. I will pay no attention to the voice of nature and to the promptings of self-love. Before each important action, I will stop to consider for a moment what relationship it has to eternal life and what may be the main reason for my undertaking it: is it for the glory of God, or for the good of my own soul, or for the good of the souls of others? If my heart says yes, then I will not swerve from carrying out the given action, unmindful of either obstacles or sacrifices. I will not be frightened into abandoning my intention. It is enough for me to know that it is pleasing to God. On the other hand, if I learn that the action has nothing in common with what I have just mentioned, I will try to elevate it to a loftier sphere by means of a good intention. And if I learn that something flows from my self-love, I will cancel it out right from the start. (1549)

Acts of Hope

My Jesus, my strength and my only hope, in You alone is all my hope. My trust will not be frustrated. (746)

… "Do what You will with me, O Jesus, I will adore You in everything. May Your will be done in me, O my Lord and my God, and I will praise Your infinite mercy." … I see that God never tries us beyond what we are able to suffer. Oh, I fear nothing; if God sends such great suffering to a soul. He upholds it with an even greater grace, although we are not aware of it. One act of trust at such moments gives greater glory to God than whole hours passed in prayer filled with consolations. (78)

O my God, my only hope, I have placed all my trust in You, and I know I shall not be disappointed. (317)

Acts of Charity

My Master, cause my heart never to expect help from anyone, but I will always strive to bring assistance, consolation and all manner of relief to others. My heart is always open to the sufferings of others; and I will not close my heart to the sufferings of others, even though because of this I have been scornfully nicknamed "dump"; that is, [because] everyone dumps his pain into my heart. [To this] I answered that everyone has a place in my heart and I, in return, have a place in the Heart of Jesus. Taunts regarding the law of love will not narrow my heart. My soul is always sensitive on this point, and Jesus alone is the motive for my love of neighbor. (871)

My Heart Is Always with You

Oh, who will comprehend Your love and Your unfathomable mercy toward us! O Prisoner of Love, I lock up my poor heart in this tabernacle, that it may adore You without cease night and day. I know of no obstacle in this adoration, and even though I be physically distant, my heart is always with You. Nothing can put a stop to my love for You. No obstacles exist for me. O my Jesus, I will console You for all the ingratitude, the blasphemies, the coldness, the hatred of the wicked, the sacrileges. O Jesus, I want to burn as a pure offering and to be consumed before the throne of Your hiddenness. I plead with You unceasingly for poor dying sinners. (80)

A Litany of Gratitude

Thank You, O God, for all the graces
Which unceasingly You lavish upon me.
Graces which enlighten me with the brilliance of the sun.
For by them You show me the sure way.

Thank You, O Lord, for creating me,
For calling me into being from nothingness,
For imprinting Your divinity on my soul,
The work of sheer merciful love.

Thank You, O God, for Holy Baptism
Which engrafted me into Your family,
A gift great beyond all thought or expression
Which transforms my soul.

Thank You, O Lord, for Holy Confession,
For that inexhaustible spring of great mercy,
For the inconceivable fountain of graces
In which sin-tainted souls become purified.

Thank You, O Jesus, for Holy Communion
In which You give us Yourself.
I feel Your Heart beating within my breast
As You cause Your divine life to unfold within me.

Thank You, O Holy Spirit, for the Sacrament of Confirmation,
Which dubs me Your knight
And gives strength to my soul at each moment,
Protecting me from evil.

Thank You, O God, for the grace of a vocation
For being called to serve you alone,
Leading me to make You my sole love,
An unequal honor for my soul.

Thank You, O Lord, for perpetual vows,
For that union of pure love,
For having deigned to unite Your pure heart with mine
And uniting my heart to Yours in the purest of bonds.

Thank You, O Lord, for the Sacrament of Anointing
Which, in my final moments will give me strength;
My help in battle, my guide to salvation,
Fortifying my soul till we rejoice forever.

Thank You, O God, for all the inspirations
That your goodness lavishes upon me,
For the interior lights given my soul,
Which the heart senses, but words cannot express.

Thank You, O Holy Trinity, for the vastness of the graces
Which you have lavished on me unceasingly through life.
My gratitude will intensify as the eternal dawn rises,
When, for the first time, I sing to Your glory. (1286)

PART III
Supplications to Our Lady of Mercy

St. Faustina understood that to love Jesus we must have a sincere love for His mother! Our Lord instructed St. Faustina to "Pray with all your heart in union with Mary" (32).

St. Faustina had a special devotion to Our Lady. In her booklet *The Spirituality of Saint Faustina*, Sister Elzbieta Siepak noted: "Sister Faustina's relationship with the Most Blessed Mother was extremely loving and close, based on the great intimacy that can only exist between the tenderest Mother and Her loving daughter."

St. Faustina wrote: "The more I imitate the Mother of God, the more deeply I get to know God" (843).

The Blessed Virgin is the Mediator and Intercessor for God's people. Her patience, sweetness, and motherly pity extend toward the holy souls in purgatory. Through her they continually receive comfort and consolation.

Our Lady cooperated in God's redemptive plan through her "yes." St. Faustina understood that "[i]t is impossible for one to please God without obeying His holy will" (1244).

Stay close to the Blessed Mother to fulfill the will of God.

Not only is Mary the Mother of Mercy, which she obtained in the highest degree, but also the mercy which God grants to people through her!

St. Faustina wrote:

Through Her, as through pure crystal,
Your mercy was passed on to us.
Through Her, man became pleasing to God;
Through Her, streams of grace flowed down upon us. (1746)

The holy souls in purgatory receive the greatest consolation from the Mother of God. She is the consoler of the afflicted — and what affliction can be greater than being a suffering soul in purgatory? She is called the Mother of Mercy, and the holy souls in purgatory refer to her as "The Star of the Sea" (20), bringing them refreshment to hasten their relief.

Consecration to Mary

To give worthy praise to the Lord's mercy,
We unite ourselves with Your Immaculate Mother,
For then our hymn will be more pleasing to You,
Because She is chosen from among men and angels. (1746)

O Mary, my Mother and my Lady, I offer You my soul, my body, my life and my death, and all that will follow it. I place everything in Your hands. O my Mother, cover my soul with Your virginal mantle and grant me the grace of purity of heart, soul and body. Defend me with Your power against all enemies and especially against those who hide their malice behind the mask of virtue. O lovely lily! You are for me a mirror, O my Mother! (79) Fortify my soul that pain may not break it. Mother of grace, teach me to live by [the power of] God. (315)

Three Virtues Dearest to Mary

Our Lady was an ever-present source of strength for St. Faustina as the nun experienced trials, sufferings, and purifications. The Virgin Mary instructed St. Faustina on her own most distinctive virtues:

I desire, My dearly beloved daughter, that you practice the three virtues that are dearest to Me — and most pleasing to God. The first is humility, humility, and once again humility; the second virtue, purity; the third virtue, love of God. As My daughter you must especially radiate with these virtues. (1415)

Imitate and practice these three virtues as they will lead us to Jesus.

LOOK TO GOD AND BE RADIANT

I sought the LORD, and he answered me,
and delivered me from all my fears.
Look to him, and be radiant;
so your faces shall never be ashamed.
This poor man cried, and the LORD heard him,
and saved him out of all his troubles.

— Psalm 34:4-6

"True radiance is about authentic beauty, but ultimately it's about an intimate connection with God in our souls. As we grow in virtue and live increasingly for God, his love radiates out through our lives and helps to heal the world."

— Lisa Mladinich, *True Radiance: Finding Grace in the Second Half of Life*

Sea of Graces to a Humble Soul

O humility, lovely flower, I see how few souls possess you. Is it because you are so beautiful and at the same time so difficult to attain? O yes, it is both the one and the other. Even God takes great pleasure in her. The floodgates of heaven are open to a humble soul, and a sea of graces flows down upon her. O how beautiful is a humble soul! From her heart, as from a censer, rises a varied and most pleasing fragrance which breaks through the skies and reaches God Himself, filling His Most Sacred Heart with joy. God refuses nothing to such a soul; she is all-powerful and influences the destiny of the whole world. God raises such a soul up to His very throne, and the more she humbles herself, the more God stoops down to her, pursuing her with His graces and accompanying her at every moment with His omnipotence. Such a soul is most deeply united with God. O humility, strike deep roots in my whole being. O Virgin most pure, but also most humble, help me to attain deep humility. Now I understand why there are so few saints; it is because so few souls are deeply humble. (1306)

St. Joseph Prayer for Purity

St. Joseph, father and guardian of virgins, into whose faithful keeping were entrusted innocence itself, Christ Jesus, and Mary, the Virgin of virgins. I pray and beseech you, through Jesus and Mary, those pledges so dear to you, to keep me from all uncleanness, and to grant that my mind may be untainted, my heart pure, and my body chaste. Help me always to serve Jesus and Mary in perfect chastity. Amen.

———

Heart of Jesus, Fount of all purity, have mercy on us.

TRUE GREATNESS IS TO LOVE GOD

"Love, love and once again, love of God — there is nothing greater in heaven or on earth. The greatest greatness is to love God; true greatness is in loving God; real wisdom is to love God. All that is great and beautiful is in God; there is no beauty or greatness outside of Him. (990) I would like to cry out to the whole world, 'Love God, because He is good and great is His mercy!'" (1372)

Prayers for Love of God

Set on Fire My Love for You!

Most sweet Jesus, set on fire my love for You and transform me into Yourself. Divinize me that my deeds may be pleasing to You. May this be accomplished by the power of the Holy Communion which I receive daily. (1289)

A Garden of Fragrant Flowers

O Supreme Good, I want to love You as no one on earth has ever loved You before! I want to adore You with every moment of my life and unite my will closely to Your holy will. My life is not drab or monotonous, but it is varied like a garden of fragrant flowers, so that I don't know which flower to pick first, the lily of suffering or the rose of love of neighbor or the violet of humility. I will not enumerate these treasures in which my every day abounds. It is a great thing to know how to make use of the present moment. (296)

Mary's Sorrows

St. Faustina had a deep devotion to Mary, the Mother of Mercy, and she meditated on the mysteries of Our Lady. Reflecting on Mary at the foot of the cross, she witnessed her tremendous love for mankind and her wanting to lead all to Jesus.

Our Lady never leaves us or the holy souls alone in our sufferings. St. Faustina wrote that Mary said to her:

> I feel constant compassion for you. (805) I sympathize with you. (635) I know how much you suffer but do not be afraid. I share with you your suffering, and I shall always do so. (25)

Mary's Sword of Suffering

The Blessed Virgin underwent horrible suffering on earth. Look to Mary for your source of strength and comfort as St. Faustina did. Comfort the holy souls with prayers for Our Lady's intercession.

> O Mary, today a terrible sword has pierced Your holy soul. Except for God, no one knows of Your suffering. Your soul does not break; it is brave, because it is with Jesus. Sweet Mother, unite my soul to Jesus, because it is only then that I will be able to endure all trials and tribulations, and only in union with Jesus will my little sacrifices be pleasing to God. Sweetest Mother, continue to teach me about the interior life. May the sword of suffering never break me. O pure Virgin, pour courage into my heart and guard it. (915)

The Seven Sorrows of Mary for the Faithful Departed

1. Mary accepts, in faith, the prophecy of Simeon.

"Behold, this child is set for the fall and rising of many in Israel, and for a sign that is spoken against (and a sword will pierce through your own soul also), that thoughts out of many hearts may be revealed" (Lk 2:34-35).

Heavenly Father, for the sake of Christ's sorrowful Passion — and the sorrows of Mary, His Mother — have mercy on the souls in purgatory.

Our Father, Hail Mary, Glory Be.

2. Mary flees into Egypt with Jesus and Joseph.

"Now when they had departed, behold, an angel of the Lord appeared to Joseph in a dream and said, 'Rise, take the child and his mother, and flee to Egypt, and remain there till I tell you; for Herod is about to search for the child, to destroy him.' And he rose and took the child and his mother by night, and departed to Egypt" (Mt 2:13-14).

Heavenly Father, for the sake of Christ's sorrowful Passion — and the sorrows of Mary, His Mother — have mercy on the souls in purgatory.

Our Father, Hail Mary, Glory Be.

3. Mary, with Joseph, seeks Jesus lost in Jerusalem.

"And when the feast was ended, as they were returning, the boy Jesus stayed behind in Jerusalem. His parents did not know it, but supposing him to be in the company they went a day's journey, and they sought him among their kinsfolk and acquaintances; and when they did not find him, they returned to Jerusalem, seeking him" (Lk 2:43-45).

Heavenly Father, for the sake of Christ's sorrowful Passion — and the sorrows of Mary, His Mother — have mercy on the souls in purgatory.

Our Father, Hail Mary, Glory Be.

4. Mary meets Jesus on the way to Calvary.

"And as they led him away, they seized one Simon of Cyrene, who was coming in from the country, and laid on him the cross, to carry it behind Jesus. And there followed him a great multitude of the people, and of women who bewailed and lamented him" (Lk 23:26-27).

Heavenly Father, for the sake of Christ's sorrowful Passion — and the sorrows of Mary, His Mother — have mercy on the souls in purgatory.

Our Father, Hail Mary, Glory Be.

5. Mary stands near the cross of her Son.

"But standing by the cross of Jesus were his mother, and his mother's sister, Mary the wife of Clopas, and Mary Magdalene. When Jesus saw his mother, and the disciple whom he loved standing near, he said to his mother, 'Woman, behold, your son!' Then he said to the disciple, 'Behold, your mother!' And from that hour the disciple took her to his own home" (Jn 19:25-27).

Heavenly Father, for the sake of Christ's sorrowful Passion — and the sorrows of Mary, His Mother — have mercy on the souls in purgatory.

Our Father, Hail Mary, Glory Be.

6. Mary receives the body of Jesus taken down from the cross.

"When it was evening, there came a rich man from Arimathea, named Joseph, who also was a disciple of Jesus. He went to Pilate and asked for the body of Jesus. Then Pilate ordered it to be given to him. And Joseph took the body, and wrapped it in a clean linen shroud" (Mt 27:57-59).

Heavenly Father, for the sake of Christ's sorrowful Passion — and the sorrows of Mary, His Mother — have mercy on the souls in purgatory.

Our Father, Hail Mary, Glory Be.

7. Mary places the body of Jesus in the tomb, awaiting the Resurrection.

"They took the body of Jesus, and bound it in linen cloths with the spices, as is the burial custom of the Jews. Now in the place where he was crucified there was a garden, and in the garden a new tomb where no one had ever been laid. So because of the Jewish day of Preparation, as the tomb was close at hand, they laid Jesus there" (Jn 19:40-42).

Heavenly Father, for the sake of Christ's sorrowful Passion — and the sorrows of Mary, His Mother — have mercy on the souls in purgatory.

Our Father, Hail Mary, Glory Be.

———

Dear Jesus, joining my prayer with the prayers of Your beloved Mother, the Star of the Sea, and with Your beloved, St. Faustina, "I plead with You for the souls that are most in need of prayer. I plead for the dying; be merciful to them. I also beg You, Jesus, to free all souls from purgatory" (240). Amen.

Prayer to Our Lady of Pity
(by St. Alphonsus Liguori)

O Lady of Pity, consoler of the afflicted and Mother of all who believe, look mercifully on the poor souls in purgatory who are also your children and more worthy of your pity because of their incapacity to help themselves in the midst of their ineffable sufferings. Pray, dear Co-Redemptrix, intercede for us with the power of your mediation before the Throne of Divine Mercy and in payment for their debt offer up the Life, Passion, and Death of Your Divine Son, together with your merits and those of all the saints in Heaven and the just on earth, so that, with divine justice completely satisfied, they may come into Paradise soon to thank and praise you forever and ever. Amen.

The Divine Mercy Rosary for the Holy Souls

St. Faustina treasured the Rosary. She prayed it while walking (especially in the cemetery) and while working in the garden. She knew its power and grace, as well as its special protection, especially for the dying and the holy souls in purgatory. She wrote:

> I prepared [for the feast of the Immaculate Conception] not only by means of the novena said in common by the whole community, but I also made a personal effort to salute Her a thousand times each day, saying a thousand "Hail Marys" for nine days in Her praise.
>
> This is now the third time I have said such a novena to the Mother of God; that is, a novena made up of a thousand Aves each day. Thus the novena consists in nine thousand salutations. Although I have done this now three times in my life, and two of these while in the course of my duties, I have never failed in carrying out my tasks with the greatest exactitude. I have always said the novena outside the time

of my exercises; that is to say, I have not said the Aves during Holy Mass or Benediction. Once, I made the novena while lying ill in the hospital. Where there's a will, there's a way. Apart from recreation, I have only prayed and worked. I have not said a single unnecessary word during these days. Although I must admit that such a matter requires a good deal of attention and effort, nothing is too much when it comes to honoring the Immaculate Virgin. (1413)

When we pray the Rosary, which is a most powerful form of mental and vocal prayer for the holy souls in purgatory, we gain fresh intercessors and increase God's glory. It is among the greatest works we can do on earth. Not only do we offer up the prayers of the Rosary for the suffering souls but also the indulgences attached to these prayers. The glory and the power of the Rosary create an amazing and effective way to gain the release of the holy souls who await our prayers.

THE POWER OF MARY

"I saw the heart of the Virgin Mother so bathed by rivers of grace flowing out from the Blessed Trinity that I understood the privilege Mary has of being the most powerful after God the Father, the wisest after God the Son, and the most benign after God the Holy Spirit."

— St. Gertrude the Great

The Joyful Mysteries

The Annunciation
He came down from heaven, forsaking th'eternal See's throne,
And assumed from Your Heart Body and Blood,

Hiding for nine months in the Virgin's Heart....

O Mother Virgin — most beautiful Lily,
Your Heart was for Jesus the first tabernacle on earth. (161)

Our Father, ten Hail Marys, Glory Be.

———

Merciful Jesus, show me nothing is impossible for You.

The Visitation

When out of love Mary went to serve her cousin Elizabeth, the child in Elizabeth's womb leapt as he recognized the divine child in Mary's womb (see Lk 1:41-44).

Today during adoration, the Lord gave me to know how much He desires a soul to distinguish itself by deeds of love. And in spirit I saw how many souls are calling out ... "Give us God." (1249)

Our Father, ten Hail Marys, Glory Be.

———

Merciful Jesus, help me believe that Your promises will be fulfilled.

The Nativity

When I started the Holy Hour, I wanted to immerse myself in the agony of Jesus in the Garden of Olives. Then I heard a voice in my soul: Meditate on the mystery of the Incarnation. And suddenly the Infant Jesus appeared before me, radiant with beauty. He told me how much God is pleased with simplicity in a soul. *[Then He said:]* Although my greatness is beyond understanding, I commune only with those who are little. I demand of you a childlike spirit. (332)

Our Father, ten Hail Marys, Glory Be.

———

Merciful Jesus, let me ponder in my heart all that You are doing in my life.

The Presentation

When Simeon recognized the baby Jesus in the Temple, he predicted Mary's sufferings (see Lk 2:35).

In the evening, I saw the Mother of God, with Her breast bared and pierced with a sword. (686) O Mary, today a terrible sword has pierced Your holy soul. Except for God, no one knows of Your suffering. (915)

Our Father, ten Hail Marys, Glory Be.

———

Merciful Jesus, give me Your revealing Light and saving Glory.

SIGNS OF CLEMENCY, TOKENS OF CHARITY

"Now man can approach God with confidence, since in the Son he has a mediator of his case with the Father, and with the Son he has [a mediatrix] in the Mother. Christ, his side laid bare [*ostentatio vulnerum*], shows the Father his side and his wounds; Mary shows Christ her womb and her breasts [*ostentatio mammarum*]; and there is no way man's case can be rejected where these monuments of clemency and tokens of charity are found together, making a request more eloquently than any tongue."

— Arnold of Bonneval (d. 1156),
Abbot of Bonneval in the Diocese of Chartres

Finding Jesus in the Temple

After Mary and Joseph found the boy Jesus in the Temple, He returned to Nazareth and was obedient to them (see Lk 2:51). So the Lord of the Universe gave us an example by obeying His humble parents!

I became absorbed in prayer and said my penance. Then I suddenly saw the Lord, who said to me, My daughter, know that you give Me greater glory by a single act of obedience than by long prayers and mortifications. Oh, how good it is to live under obedience, to live conscious of the fact that everything I do is pleasing to God! (894)

Our Father, ten Hail Marys, Glory Be.

———

Merciful Jesus, assist me in carrying out our Father's business.

The Luminous Mysteries

The Baptism of Our Lord

When the Lord allowed John the Baptist to submerge Him in the Jordan, He sanctified the waters for our baptism.

Through Holy Baptism, we entered into union with other souls. Death tightens the bonds of love. I ought always to be of help to others. If I am a good religious, I will be useful, not only to the Order, but to the whole Country as well. (391)

Our Father, ten Hail Marys, Glory Be.

———

Merciful Jesus, help me repent and believe in your Gospel.

The Wedding Feast at Cana

Jesus' presence at the wedding feast at Cana anticipated His attendance at the wedding feast of the Eucharist.

Today, my soul is preparing for Holy Communion as for a wedding feast, wherein all the participants are resplendent with unspeakable beauty. And, I, too, have been invited to this banquet, but I do not see that beauty within myself, only an abyss of misery. And, although I do not feel worthy of sitting down to table, I will however slip under the table, at the feet of Jesus, and will beg for the crumbs that fall from the table. Knowing Your mercy, I therefore approach You, Jesus, for sooner will I run out of misery than will the compassion of Your Heart exhaust itself. That is why during this day I will keep arousing trust in The Divine Mercy. (1827)

Our Father, ten Hail Marys, Glory Be.

———

Merciful Jesus, direct me to do whatever You tell me.

The Proclamation of the Kingdom

The Lord Jesus proclaimed the coming of the Kingdom and commissioned us to continue His work.

The Lord gave me to know, during meditation, that as long as my heart beats in my breast, I must always strive to spread the Kingdom of God on earth, I am to fight for the glory of my Creator. (1548)

[Jesus said:] But child, you are not yet in your homeland; so go, fortified, by My grace, and fight for My Kingdom in human souls; fight as a king's child would; and remember that the days of your exile will pass quickly, and with them the possibility of earning merit for

heaven. I expect from you, My child, a great number of souls who will glorify My mercy for all eternity. (1489)

Our Father, ten Hail Marys, Glory Be.

———

Merciful Jesus, be God's Kingdom for me and all Your people.

The Transfiguration

On one occasion I was reflecting on the Holy Trinity, on the essence of God. I absolutely wanted to know and fathom who God is. … In an instant my spirit was caught up into what seemed to be the next world. I saw an inaccessible light, and in this light what appeared like three sources of light which I could not understand. And out of that light came words in the form of lightning which encircled heaven and earth. Not understanding anything, I was very sad. Suddenly, from this sea of inaccessible light came our dearly beloved Savior, unutterably beautiful with His shining Wounds. And from this light came a voice which said, Who God is in His Essence, no one will fathom, neither the mind of Angels nor of man. Jesus said to me, Get to know God by contemplating His attributes. (30)

Our Father, ten Hail Marys, Glory Be.

———

Merciful Jesus, manifest Yourself to me however you wish.

The Institution of the Eucharist

At the Last Supper, when Jesus instituted the Eucharist, His disciples remembered His promise that whoever eats His body and drinks His blood will have eternal life (see Jn 6:54).

Every morning during meditation, I prepare myself for the whole day's struggle. Holy Communion assures me that I will win the victory; and so it is. I fear the day when I do not receive Holy Communion. This Bread of the Strong gives me all the strength I need to carry on my mission and the courage to do whatever the Lord asks of me. The courage and strength that are in me are not of me, but of Him who lives in me — it is the Eucharist. (91)

Our Father, ten Hail Marys, Glory Be.

———

Merciful Jesus, change me into a witness of Your love.

The Sorrowful Mysteries

The Agony in the Garden

In the evening, when I entered the small chapel, I heard these words in my soul: My daughter, consider these words: "And being in agony, he prayed more earnestly." When I started to think about them more deeply, much light streamed into my soul. I learned how much we need perseverance in prayer and that our salvation often depends on such difficult prayer. (157)

A soul arms itself by prayer for all kinds of combat. In whatever state the soul may be, it ought to pray. A soul which is pure and beautiful must pray, or else it will lose its beauty; a soul which is striving after this purity must pray, or else it will never attain it; a soul which is newly converted must pray, or else it will fall again; a sinful soul plunged in sins, must pray so that it might rise again. There is no soul which is not bound to pray, for every single grace comes to the soul through prayer. (146)

Our Father, ten Hail Marys, Glory Be.

———

Merciful Jesus, enable me to do Your will and not my own.

The Scourging at the Pillar

I saw the Lord Jesus tied to a pillar, stripped of His clothes, and the scourging began immediately. I saw four men who took turns at striking the Lord with scourges. My heart almost stopped at the sight of these tortures. The Lord said to me, I suffer even greater pain than that which you see. And Jesus gave me to know for what sins He subjected Himself to the scourging: these are sins of impurity. Oh, how dreadful was Jesus' moral suffering during the scourging! Then Jesus said to me, Look and see the human race in its present condition. In an instant, I saw horrible things: the executioners left Jesus, and other people started scourging Him; they seized the scourges and struck the Lord mercilessly. These were priests, religious men and women, and high dignitaries of the Church, which surprised me greatly. There were lay people of all ages and walks of life. All vented their malice on the innocent Jesus. Seeing this, my heart fell as if into a mortal agony. (445)

Our Father, ten Hail Marys, Glory Be.

———

Merciful Jesus, involve me in Your suffering for my sins.

The Crowning with Thorns

In the morning, during meditation, I felt a painful thorn in the left side of my head. The suffering continued all day. I meditated continually about how Jesus had been able to endure the pain of so many thorns which made up His crown. I joined my suffering to the sufferings of Jesus and offered it for sinners. (349)

I felt His pain, so terrible that we have not the faintest idea of how much He suffered for us before He was crucified. My soul was filled with pain and longing; in my soul, I felt great hatred for sin, and even the smallest infidelity on my part seemed to me like a huge mountain for which I must expiate by mortification and penance. When I see Jesus tormented, my heart is torn to pieces, and I think: what will become of sinners if they do not take advantage of the Passion of Jesus: In His Passion, I see a whole sea of mercy. (948)

Our Father, ten Hail Marys, Glory Be.

———

Merciful Jesus, share with me Your passion's sorrow.

The Carrying of the Cross

Then I saw the Lord Jesus nailed to the cross. When He had hung on it for a while, I saw the multitude of souls crucified like Him. Then I saw a second multitude of souls, and a third. The second multitude was not nailed to [their] crosses, but were holding them firmly in their hands. The third were neither nailed to [their] crosses nor holding them firmly in their hands, but were dragging [their] crosses behind them and were discontent. Jesus then said to me: Do you see these souls? Those who are like Me in the pain and contempt they suffer will be like Me in glory. And those who resemble me less in pain and contempt will also bear less resemblance to Me in glory. (446)

I have learned that the greatest power is hidden in patience. I see that patience always leads to victory, although not immediately; but that victory will become manifest after many years. Patience is linked to meekness. (1514)

Our Father, ten Hail Marys, Glory Be.

———

Merciful Jesus, allow me to take up my cross and follow You.

The Crucifixion

All at once, I saw the image in some small chapel and at that moment I saw that the chapel became an enormous and beautiful temple. And in this temple I saw the Mother of God with the Infant in Her arms. And a moment later, the Infant Jesus disappeared from the arms of His Mother, and I saw the living image of Jesus Crucified. The Mother of God told me to do what She had done, that, even when joyful, I should always keep my eyes fixed on the cross.... (561)

> "We resemble God most when we forgive our neighbors. God is Love, Goodness, and Mercy.... He who knows how to forgive prepares for himself many graces from God. As often as I look upon the cross, so often will I forgive with all my heart." (1148, 390)

[L]et every soul trust in the Passion of the Lord, and place its hope in His mercy. God will not deny His mercy to anyone. Heaven and earth may change, but God's mercy will never be exhausted. (72)

[Jesus to St. Faustina:] My daughter, today consider my Sorrowful Passion in all its immensity. Consider it as if it had been undertaken for your sake alone. (1761)

Our Father, ten Hail Marys, Glory Be.

———

Merciful Jesus, grant me a holy death and eternal peace. I trust in You.

The Glorious Mysteries

The Resurrection

Today, during the [Mass of the] Resurrection, I saw the Lord Jesus in the midst of a great light. He approached me and said, Peace be to you, My children, and He lifted up His hand and gave His blessing. The wounds in His hands, feet and side were indelible and shining. When He looked at me with such kindness and love, my whole soul drowned itself in Him. And He said to me, You have taken a great part in My Passion; therefore, I now give you a great share in my joy and glory. The whole time of the Resurrection [Mass] seemed like only a minute to me. A wondrous recollection filled my soul and lasted throughout the whole festal season. The kindness of Jesus is so great that I cannot express it. (205)

Our Father, ten Hail Marys, Glory Be.

———

Merciful Jesus, raise me up body and soul on the last day.

The Ascension

May 26 [1938 — feast of the Ascension]. Today I accompanied the Lord Jesus as He ascended into heaven. It was about noon. I was overcome by a great longing for God. It is a strange thing, the more I felt God's presence, the more ardently I desired Him. Then I saw myself in the midst of a huge crowd of disciples and apostles, together with the Mother of God. Jesus was telling them to ... Go out into the whole world and teach in My name. He stretched out His hands and blessed them and disappeared in a cloud. I saw the longing of Our Lady. Her soul yearned for Jesus, with the whole force of Her love. But she was so peaceful and so united to the will of God that there was not a stir in her heart but for what God wanted. (1710)

Our Father, ten Hail Marys, Glory Be.

———

Merciful Jesus, be with me always until the end of my time.

The Descent of the Holy Spirit
After Jesus returned to His Father, He poured out the Holy Spirit on His disciples and on us.

Be adored, O Most Holy Trinity, now and for all time. Be adored in all Your works and all Your creatures. May the greatness of Your mercy be admired and glorified, O God. (5)

O Holy Trinity, in whom is contained the inner life of God, the Father, the Son, and the Holy Spirit, eternal joy, inconceivable depth of love, poured out upon all creatures and constituting their happiness, honor and glory be to Your holy name forever and ever. Amen. (525)

Our Father, ten Hail Marys, Glory Be.

———

Merciful Jesus, send out your Holy Spirit into our world.

The Assumption

On the day of the Assumption of the Mother of God ... I saw the Mother of God, unspeakably beautiful. She said to me, My daughter, what I demand from you is prayer, prayer, and once again prayer, for the world and especially for your country. For nine days receive Holy Communion in atonement and unite yourself closely to the Holy Sacrifice of the Mass. During these nine days you will stand before God as an offering; always and everywhere, at all times and places, day or night, whenever you wake up, pray in the spirit. In spirit, one can always remain in prayer. (325)

Our Father, ten Hail Marys, Glory Be.

———

Merciful Jesus, teach me to pray with the Church at all times.

The Coronation of Mary in Heaven

I am not only the Queen of Heaven, but also the Mother of Mercy and your Mother. (330) I am Mother to you all, thanks to the unfathomable mercy of God. Most pleasing to me is that soul which faithfully carries out the will of God. (449)

Our Father, ten Hail Marys, Glory Be.

———

Merciful Jesus, continue to permit Mary to bring us to You.

Mary, My Shield and Defense

St. Faustina refers to Our Lady's mantle as a refuge of mercy. Mary serves as a reflection of God and as our mother and shield because God gives His protection through the Virgin Mary.

———

August Queen of Heaven, heavenly sovereign of the Angels, you who from the beginning received from God the power and the mission to crush the head of Satan, we humbly beseech you to send your holy legions, so that under your command and through your power, they may pursue the demons and combat them everywhere, suppress their boldness, and drive them back into the abyss. Who is like God? O good and tender Mother, you will always be our love and hope! O Divine Mother, send your holy angels to defend me and to drive far away from me the cruel enemy.

Holy Angels and Archangels, defend us, guard us. Amen.

Mary, The Dawn

O sweet Mother of God,
I model my life on You;
You are for me the bright dawn;
In You I lose myself, enraptured.

O Mother Immaculate Virgin,
In You the divine ray is reflected,
Midst storms, 'tis You who teach me to love the Lord,
O my shield and defense from the foe. (1232)

O my Mother, cover my soul with Your virginal mantle.... (79)

PART IV
Novenas, Litanies, and Selected Prayers

"God Is Rich in Mercy" Novena for the Suffering Souls

In his encyclical *Dives in Misericordia* (DM; *Rich in Mercy*), St. John Paul II called mercy the "second name of love" and the greatest attribute of God toward all mankind. He wrote, "[T]he Church must consider it one of her principal duties — at every stage of history and especially in our modern age — to proclaim and to introduce into life the mystery of mercy, supremely revealed in Jesus Christ" (DM 24).

Jesus taught St. Faustina about the mystery of His mercy and His desire for her heart to be a channel of His mercy. Our hearts are to be an abiding place of His mercy.

In this spirit, let us pray a novena of mercy for the suffering souls who are in desperate need of our prayers. Remember, they can no longer merit. They rely on our mercy!

Day One

The Revelation of Mercy of He Who Sees The Father

Jesus' message is that God is rich in mercy. Although none of us have seen God, we can experience His love through Christ. This is so important today when we attempt to master the earth but are beset with anxiety.

The truth revealed in Christ, about God the "Father of Mercies," enables us "to see" Him as particularly close to man especially when man is suffering, when he is under threat at the very heart of his existence and dignity. (DM 2)

———

King of Mercy, guide my soul.

Day Two

The Messianic Message

Jesus preached that God the Father is ever present in the world as love and mercy, especially toward the poor, the disabled, those suffering from injustice, and sinners.

Especially through His lifestyle and through His actions, Jesus revealed that love is present in the world in which we live.... At the same time [He] demanded from people that they also should be guided in their lives by love and mercy. (DM 3)

———

King of Mercy, guide my soul.

Day Three

The Concept of "Mercy" in the Old Testament

God shows His mercy in the Old Testament toward His chosen people, the Jews, despite their sins, infidelities, and betrayals. Although men's justice in confronting sin is a virtue, it is transcended by God's love and forgiveness.

The Old Testament encourages people suffering from misfortune, especially those weighed down by sin ... to appeal for mercy and enables them to count upon it. (DM 4)

———

King of Mercy, guide my soul.

Day Four

The Parable of the Prodigal Son

The prodigal son represents every man who has squandered his inheritance of grace and original justice.

The inheritance that the son had received from his father was a quantity of material goods, but more important than these goods was his dignity as a son in his father's house.... [Justice would demand that the son be treated as his father's servant but the father] "had compassion, ran to meet him, threw his arms around his neck, and kissed him" [Lk 15:20]." (DM 5, 6)

—

King of Mercy, guide my soul.

Day Five

The Paschal Mystery

The Paschal Mystery is the unfolding story of God's infinite love and mercy expressed in the suffering, death, and resurrection of His Son. It promises eternal life to those who obey God's commandments and embody love and mercy in their own lives and toward others.

The love of the Father which is more powerful than death ... [and] is to be everlastingly confirmed as more powerful than sin. (DM 8)

—

King of Mercy, guide my soul.

Day Six

Mercy from Generation to Generation

Our own time is unique in terms of scientific progress, as well as the awareness of the inter-relatedness of mankind. Yet suffering, evil, and death persist. Modern man lives in a paradox. Scientific technological progress brings us wonder, controls over nature, instant communication, and awareness of the laws of human behavior. At the same time, the possibility of nuclear annihilation hangs like a scythe over us. Inequalities increase and millions die of hunger. Man's justice to remedy these evils is not enough; it can be vindictive and dehumanizing.

Human action can deviate from justice itself, even when it is being undertaken in the name of justice. (DM 12)

———

King of Mercy, guide my soul.

Day Seven

The Mercy of God in the Mission of the Church

It is the Church's mission to proclaim God's mercy and embody it in the lives of the faithful and in all people of good will. It is the Church's duty to appeal to God's infinite mercy and love through ardent and passionate prayer.

Also infinite therefore and inexhaustible is the Father's readiness to receive the prodigal children who return to His home. Infinite are the readiness and power of forgiveness which flow continually from the marvelous value of the sacrifice of the Son. (DM 13)

———

King of Mercy, guide my soul.

Day Eight

The Prayer of the Church in Our Times

Modern man is threatened and anxious. As the world succumbs to secularization, we lose the meaning of mercy. We must constantly keep in mind God's mercy, which is not man's justice, but superior to it.

[God's mercy] is love of people, of all men and women without any exception or division: without difference of race, culture, language, or world outlook, without distinction between friends and enemies. (DM 15)

———

King of Mercy, guide my soul.

Day Nine

Love and Mercy in Our Lives Day by Day

We are always tempted by sin, yet every day gives us the opportunity to express — however imperfectly — God's love and mercy toward our fellow man. In the ordinary, the mundane, and the commonplace, we can reach out to our brothers and sisters and together walk the path to absolution and eternal life.

"Blessed are the merciful, they shall obtain mercy." (Mt 5:7)

———

King of Mercy, guide my soul.

Divine Mercy Litany to St. Faustina

Lord, have mercy. Christ, have mercy. Lord, have mercy.

Christ, hear us. Christ, graciously hear us.

God the Father of heaven — have mercy on us.

God the Son, Redeemer of the world — have mercy on us.

God, the Holy Spirit — have mercy on us.

Holy Mary — pray for us.

St. Faustina, living witness of the heavenly Father's mercy —
*   pray for us.*

St. Faustina, humble servant of Jesus, Mercy Incarnate ...

St. Faustina, obedient instrument of the Spirit, the Comforter ...

St. Faustina, trustful daughter of the Mother of Mercy ...

St. Faustina, confidante of the Divine Mercy message ...

St. Faustina, faithful secretary of the words of the Merciful Jesus ...

St. Faustina, great apostle of God's mercy ...

St. Faustina, dispenser of God rich in mercy ...

St. Faustina, gift of God for the whole world ...

St. Faustina, perceiving the goodness of the Creator to every creature ...

St. Faustina, glorifying God in the mystery of the Incarnation ...

St. Faustina, partaker in the Lord's passion and resurrection ...

St. Faustina, guide on the way of Jesus' cross ...

St. Faustina, meeting with Jesus in the holy sacraments ...

St. Faustina, united with the Spouse in your soul ...

St. Faustina, enraptured by the mercy of God in Mary's life ...

St. Faustina, loving the Church, the Mystical Body of Christ ...

St. Faustina, powerful with genuine faith ...

St. Faustina, persevering in unwavering hope ...

St. Faustina, enkindled with ardent love ...

St. Faustina, beautiful with true humility ...

St. Faustina, simple with childlike trust ...

St. Faustina, model of fulfilling God's will ...

St. Faustina, example of generous service ...

St. Faustina, caring protector of the souls of priests and religious ...

St. Faustina, defender of young people and children against evil ...

St. Faustina, hope of the fallen and the despairing ...

St. Faustina, strength of the sick and the suffering ...

St. Faustina, safeguarding trust in the hearts of the dying ...

St. Faustina, offering yourself for sinners ...

St. Faustina, solicitous for the salvation of all people ...

St. Faustina, advocate of the suffering souls in purgatory ...

St. Faustina, imploring God's mercy for the whole world ...

*Lamb of God, who takes away the sins of the world — spare us
O Lord.*

*Lamb of God, who takes away the sins of the world — graciously
hear us, O Lord.*

*Lamb of God, who takes away the sins of the world — have mercy
on us.*

V. Pray for us, St. Faustina.

*R. That we may proclaim the message of Mercy to the world with our
life and words.*

Let us pray:

*Merciful God, receive our thanksgiving for the gift of St. Faustina's life and
mission. Grant, we beseech You, that by her intercession we may grow in the*

attitude of trust in You and mercy toward our neighbor. Through Christ Our Lord. Amen.

Gaining Sanctity

God revealed to St. Faustina the understanding of what sanctity is and of what it consists. Petition Jesus for this extraordinary grace!

Neither graces, nor revelations, nor raptures, nor gifts granted to a soul make it perfect, but rather the intimate union of the soul with God. These gifts are merely ornaments of the soul, but constitute neither its essence nor its perfection. My sanctity and perfection consist in the close union of my will with the will of God. God never violates our free will. It is up to us whether we want to receive God's grace or not. It is up to us whether we will cooperate with it or waste it. (1107)

Prayer for Faithfulness to the Holy Spirit

O Jesus, keep me in holy fear, so that I may not waste graces. Help me to be faithful to the inspirations of the Holy Spirit. Grant that my heart may burst for love of You, rather than I should neglect even one act of love for You. (1557)

Novena to St. Faustina to Obtain Graces

O Jesus, who filled St. Faustina with profound veneration for Your Boundless Mercy, deign, if it be Your holy will, to grant me, through her intercession, the grace for which I fervently pray: [mention your petition]. My sins render me unworthy of Your Mercy, but be mindful of Sister Faustina's spirit of sacrifice and self-denial, and reward her virtue by granting the petition which, with childlike trust, I present to You through her intercession.

Our Father, Hail Mary, Glory Be.

St. Faustina, pray for us.

St. Faustina's Healing Prayer

Jesus, may Your pure and healthy blood circulate in my ailing organism, and may Your pure and healthy body transform my weak body, and may a healthy and vigorous life throb within me, if it is truly Your holy will…. (1089)

Prayer for the Future and Present Moment

O My God

When I look into the future, I am frightened,
But why plunge into the future?
Only the present moment is precious to me,
As the future may never enter my soul at all.

It is no longer in my power
To change, correct or add to the past;
For neither sages nor prophets could do that.
And so, what the past has embraced I must entrust to God.

O present moment, you belong to me, whole and entire.
I desire to serve you as best I can.
And although I am weak and small,
You grant me the grace of Your omnipotence.

And so, trusting in Your mercy,
I walk through life like a little child,
Offering You each day this heart
Burning with love for Your greater Glory. (2)

A Novena of Meditations and Prayers for the Holy Souls

Jesus said to St. Faustina: "I demand from you deeds of mercy, which are to rise out of love for Me. You are to show mercy to your neighbors always and everywhere. You must not shrink from this or try to excuse or absolve yourself from it" (742).

Be a reflection of God's great mercy for the sake of the holy souls.

Day One

Jesus said to St. Faustina: "Enter into purgatory often, because they need you there" (1738).

Help me, O Lord, that my eyes may be merciful, so that I may never suspect or judge from appearances, but look for what is beautiful in my neighbors' souls....

Help me, O Lord, that my ears may be merciful, so that I may give heed to my neighbors' needs....

Help me, O Lord, that my tongue may be merciful, so that I should never speak negatively of my neighbor....

Help me, O Lord, that my hands may be merciful and filled with good deeds, so that I may do only good to my neighbors....

Help me, O Lord, that my feet may be merciful, so that I may hurry to assist my neighbor....

Help me, O Lord, that my heart may be merciful, so that I myself may feel all the sufferings of my neighbor.... (163)

———

May Your mercy, O Lord, rest upon me. Amen.

Day Two

St. Faustina saw a great crowd of suffering souls. They were praying but to no avail for themselves; only we can come to their aid. "[I heard an interior voice] which said, My mercy does not want this, but justice demands it" (20).

Help me, O Lord, that my eyes may be merciful, so that I may never suspect or judge from appearances, but look for what is beautiful in my neighbors' souls....

Help me, O Lord, that my ears may be merciful, so that I may give heed to my neighbors' needs....

Help me, O Lord, that my tongue may be merciful, so that I should never speak negatively of my neighbor....

Help me, O Lord, that my hands may be merciful and filled with good deeds, so that I may do only good to my neighbors....

Help me, O Lord, that my feet may be merciful, so that I may hurry to assist my neighbor....

Help me, O Lord, that my heart may be merciful, so that I myself may feel all the sufferings of my neighbor.... (163)

———

May Your mercy, O Lord, rest upon me. Amen.

Day Three

"Good Friday. At three o'clock I saw the Lord Jesus, crucified, who looked at me and said, I thirst" (648).

Help me, O Lord, that my eyes may be merciful, so that I may never suspect or judge from appearances, but look for what is beautiful in my neighbors' souls....

Help me, O Lord, that my ears may be merciful, so that I may give heed to my neighbors' needs....

Help me, O Lord, that my tongue may be merciful, so that I should never speak negatively of my neighbor....

Help me, O Lord, that my hands may be merciful and filled with good deeds, so that I may do only good to my neighbors....

Help me, O Lord, that my feet may be merciful, so that I may hurry to assist my neighbor....

Help me, O Lord, that my heart may be merciful, so that I myself may feel all the sufferings of my neighbor.... (163)

———

May Your mercy, O Lord, rest upon me. Amen.

Day Four

Jesus said to St. Faustina: "My daughter, I want to instruct you on how you are to rescue souls through sacrifice and prayer" (1767).

Help me, O Lord, that my eyes may be merciful, so that I may never suspect or judge from appearances, but look for what is beautiful in my neighbors' souls....

Help me, O Lord, that my ears may be merciful, so that I may give heed to my neighbors' needs....

Help me, O Lord, that my tongue may be merciful, so that I should never speak negatively of my neighbor....

Help me, O Lord, that my hands may be merciful and filled with good deeds, so that I may do only good to my neighbors....

Help me, O Lord, that my feet may be merciful, so that I may hurry to assist my neighbor....

Help me, O Lord, that my heart may be merciful, so that I myself may feel all the sufferings of my neighbor.... (163)

—

May Your mercy, O Lord, rest upon me. Amen.

Day Five

Jesus said to St. Faustina: "I am giving you three ways of exercising mercy toward your neighbor: the first — by deed, the second — by word, the third — by prayer. In these three degrees is contained the fullness of mercy, and it is an unquestionable proof of love for Me.... [E]ven the strongest faith is of no avail without works" (742).

Help me, O Lord, that my eyes may be merciful, so that I may never suspect or judge from appearances, but look for what is beautiful in my neighbors' souls....

Help me, O Lord, that my ears may be merciful, so that I may give heed to my neighbors' needs....

Help me, O Lord, that my tongue may be merciful, so that I should never speak negatively of my neighbor....

Help me, O Lord, that my hands may be merciful and filled with good deeds, so that I may do only good to my neighbors....

Help me, O Lord, that my feet may be merciful, so that I may hurry to assist my neighbor....

Help me, O Lord, that my heart may be merciful, so that I myself may feel all the sufferings of my neighbor.... (163)

———

May Your mercy, O Lord, rest upon me. Amen.

Day Six

Jesus said to St. Faustina: "Is your love for your neighbor guided by My love? Do you pray for your enemies? Do you wish well to those who have, in one way or another, caused you sorrow or offended you?" (1768).

Help me, O Lord, that my eyes may be merciful, so that I may never suspect or judge from appearances, but look for what is beautiful in my neighbors' souls....

Help me, O Lord, that my ears may be merciful, so that I may give heed to my neighbors' needs....

Help me, O Lord, that my tongue may be merciful, so that I should never speak negatively of my neighbor....

Help me, O Lord, that my hands may be merciful and filled with good deeds, so that I may do only good to my neighbors....

Help me, O Lord, that my feet may be merciful, so that I may hurry to assist my neighbor....

Help me, O Lord, that my heart may be merciful, so that I myself may feel all the sufferings of my neighbor.... (163)

———

May Your mercy, O Lord, rest upon me. Amen.

Day Seven

Jesus said to St. Faustina: "Know that whatever good you do to any soul, I accept it as if you had done it to Me" (1768).

Help me, O Lord, that my eyes may be merciful, so that I may never suspect or judge from appearances, but look for what is beautiful in my neighbors' souls....

Help me, O Lord, that my ears may be merciful, so that I may give heed to my neighbors' needs....

Help me, O Lord, that my tongue may be merciful, so that I should never speak negatively of my neighbor....

Help me, O Lord, that my hands may be merciful and filled with good deeds, so that I may do only good to my neighbors....

Help me, O Lord, that my feet may be merciful, so that I may hurry to assist my neighbor....

Help me, O Lord, that my heart may be merciful, so that I myself may feel all the sufferings of my neighbor.... (163)

———

May Your mercy, O Lord, rest upon me. Amen.

Day Eight

Jesus said to St. Faustina: "Today bring to Me the souls who are in the prison of Purgatory, and immerse them in the abyss of My mercy. Let the torrents of my Blood cool down their scorching flames. All these souls are greatly loved by Me. They are making retribution to My justice. It is in your power to bring them relief" (1226).

Help me, O Lord, that my eyes may be merciful, so that I may never suspect or judge from appearances, but look for what is beautiful in my neighbors' souls....

Help me, O Lord, that my ears may be merciful, so that I may give heed to my neighbors' needs....

Help me, O Lord, that my tongue may be merciful, so that I should never speak negatively of my neighbor....

Help me, O Lord, that my hands may be merciful and filled with good deeds, so that I may do only good to my neighbors....

Help me, O Lord, that my feet may be merciful, so that I may hurry to assist my neighbor....

Help me, O Lord, that my heart may be merciful, so that I myself may feel all the sufferings of my neighbor.... (163)

———

May Your mercy, O Lord, rest upon me. Amen.

Day Nine

Jesus said to St. Faustina: "Draw all the indulgences from the treasury of My Church and offer them on their behalf. Oh, if you only knew the torments they suffer, you would continually offer for them the alms of the spirit and pay off their debt to My justice" (1226).

Help me, O Lord, that my eyes may be merciful, so that I may never suspect or judge from appearances, but look for what is beautiful in my neighbors' souls....

Help me, O Lord, that my ears may be merciful, so that I may give heed to my neighbors' needs....

Help me, O Lord, that my tongue may be merciful, so that I should never speak negatively of my neighbor....

Help me, O Lord, that my hands may be merciful and filled with good deeds, so that I may do only good to my neighbors....

Help me, O Lord, that my feet may be merciful, so that I may hurry to assist my neighbor....

Help me, O Lord, that my heart may be merciful, so that I myself may feel all the sufferings of my neighbor.... (163)

———

May Your mercy, O Lord, rest upon me. Amen.

A Novena to the Divine Mercy

First Day
Today bring to Me
all mankind especially all sinners.... (see 1210)

Most Merciful Jesus, whose very nature it is to have compassion on us and to forgive us, do not look upon our sins but upon our trust which we place in Your infinite goodness. Receive us all into the abode of Your Most Compassionate Heart, and never let us escape from It. We beg this of You by Your love which unites You to the Father and the Holy Spirit....

Eternal Father, turn Your merciful gaze upon all mankind and especially upon poor sinners, all enfolded in the Most Compassionate Heart of Jesus. For the sake of His sorrowful Passion show us Your mercy, that we may praise the omnipotence of Your mercy forever and ever. Amen. (1211)

Second Day

TODAY BRING TO ME
the souls of priests and religious.... (see 1212)

Most merciful Jesus, from whom comes all that is good, increase Your grace in us, that we may perform worthy works of mercy, and that all who see them may glorify the Father of Mercy who is in heaven....

Eternal Father, turn your merciful gaze upon the company [of chosen ones] in Your vineyard — upon the souls of priests and religious; and endow them with the strength of Your blessing. For the love of the Heart of Your Son in which they are enfolded, impart to them Your power and light, that they may be able to guide others in the way of salvation, and with one voice sing praise to Your boundless mercy for ages without end. Amen. (1213)

Third Day

TODAY BRING TO ME
all devout and faithful souls.... (see 1214)

Most Merciful Jesus, from the treasury of Your mercy You impart Your graces in great abundance to each and all. Receive us into the abode of Your Most Compassionate Heart and never let us escape from it. We beg this of You by that most wondrous love for the heavenly Father with which Your Heart burns so fiercely....

Eternal Father, turn Your merciful gaze upon faithful souls, as upon the inheritance of Your Son. For the sake of His sorrowful Passion, grant them Your blessing and surround them with Your constant protection. Thus may they never fail in love or lose the treasure of the holy faith, but rather, with all the hosts of Angels and Saints, may they glorify Your boundless mercy for endless ages. Amen. (1215)

Fourth Day
TODAY BRING TO ME
the pagans and those who do not yet know Me.... (see 1216)

Most Compassionate Jesus, You are the Light of the whole world. Receive into the abode of Your Most Compassionate Heart the souls of pagans who as yet do not know You. Let the rays of Your grace enlighten them that they, too, together with us, may extol Your wonderful mercy; and do not let them escape from the abode which is Your Most Compassionate Heart....

Eternal Father, turn Your merciful gaze upon the souls of pagans and of those who as yet do not know You, but who are enclosed in the Most Compassionate Heart of Jesus. Draw them to the light of the Gospel. These souls do not know what great happiness it is to love You. Grant that they, too, may extol the generosity of Your mercy for endless ages. Amen. (1217)

Fifth Day
TODAY BRING TO ME
the souls of the heretics and schismatics.... (see 1218)

Most Merciful Jesus, Goodness Itself, You do not refuse light to those who seek it of You. Receive into the abode of Your Most Compassionate Heart the souls of heretics and schismatics. Draw them by Your light into the unity of the Church, and do not let them escape from the abode of Your Most Compassionate Heart; but bring it about that they, too, come to extol the generosity of Your mercy....

Eternal Father, turn Your merciful gaze upon the souls of heretics and schismatics, who have squandered Your blessings and misused Your graces by obstinately persisting in their errors. Do not look upon their errors, but upon the love of Your own Son and upon His bitter Passion, which He underwent for their sake, since they, too, are enclosed in the Most Compassionate Heart of Jesus. Bring it about that they also may glorify Your great mercy for endless ages. Amen. (1219)

Sixth Day
TODAY BRING TO ME
the meek and humble souls and the souls of little children....
(see 1220)

Most Merciful Jesus, You Yourself have said, "Learn from Me for I am meek and humble of heart." Receive into the abode of Your Most Compassionate Heart all meek and humble souls and the souls of little children. These souls send all heaven into ecstasy and they are the heavenly Father's favorites. They are a sweet-smelling bouquet before the throne of God; God Himself takes delight in their fragrance. These souls have a permanent abode in Your Most Compassionate Heart, O Jesus, and they unceasingly sing out a hymn of love and mercy.... (1221)

Eternal Father, turn Your merciful gaze upon meek souls and humble souls, and upon the souls of little children who are enfolded in the abode which is the Most Compassionate Heart of Jesus. These souls bear the closest resemblance to Your Son. Their fragrance rises from the earth and reaches Your very throne. Father of mercy and of all goodness, I beg You by the love You bear these souls and by the delight

You take in them: Bless the whole world, that all souls together may sing out the praises of Your mercy for endless ages. Amen. (1223)

Seventh Day

Today bring to Me
the souls who especially venerate and glorify My mercy....
(see 1224)

Most Merciful Jesus, whose Heart is Love Itself, receive into the abode of Your Most Compassionate Heart the souls of those who particularly extol and venerate the greatness of Your mercy. These souls are mighty with the very power of God Himself. In the midst of all afflictions and adversities they go forward, confident of Your mercy. These souls are united to Jesus and carry all mankind on their shoulders. These souls will not be judged severely, but Your mercy will embrace them as they depart from this life....

Eternal Father, turn your merciful gaze upon the souls who glorify and venerate Your greatest attribute, that of Your fathomless mercy, and who are enclosed in the Most Compassionate Heart of Jesus. These souls are a living Gospel; their hands are full of deeds of mercy, and their spirit, overflowing with joy, sing a canticle of mercy to You, O Most High! I beg You O God: Show them Your mercy according to the hope and trust they have placed in You. Let there be accomplished in them the promise of Jesus, who said to them, I Myself will defend as My own glory, during their lifetime, and especially at the hour of their death, those souls who will venerate My fathomless mercy. (1225)

Eighth Day
TODAY BRING TO ME
the souls who are in the prison of Purgatory.... (see 1226)

Most Merciful Jesus, Your Yourself have said that You desire mercy; so I bring into the abode of Your Most Compassionate Heart the souls in Purgatory, souls who are very dear to You, and yet, who must make retribution to Your justice. May the streams of Blood and Water which gushed forth from Your Heart put out the flames of purifying fire, that in that place, too, the power of Your mercy may be praised....

Eternal Father, turn Your merciful gaze upon the souls suffering in Purgatory, who are enfolded in the Most Compassionate Heart of Jesus. I beg You, by the sorrowful Passion of Jesus Your Son, and by all the bitterness with which His most sacred Soul was flooded, manifest Your mercy to the souls who are under Your just scrutiny. Look upon them in no other way than through the Wounds of Jesus, Your dearly beloved Son; for we firmly believe that there is no limit to Your goodness and compassion. (1227)

Ninth Day
TODAY BRING TO ME
souls who have become lukewarm.... (see 1228)

Most Compassionate Jesus, You are Compassion Itself. I bring lukewarm souls into the abode of Your Most Compassionate Heart. In this fire of Your pure love let these tepid souls, who, like corpses, filled You with such deep loathing, be once again set aflame. O Most Compassionate Jesus, exercise the omnipotence of Your mercy and draw them into the very ardor of Your love; and bestow upon them the gift of holy love, for nothing is beyond Your power....

Eternal Father, turn Your merciful gaze upon lukewarm souls, who are nonetheless enfolded in the Most Compassionate Heart of Jesus. Father of Mercy, I beg You by the bitter Passion of Your Son and by His three-hour agony on the Cross: Let them, too, glorify the abyss of Your mercy.... (1229)

Help Me Do the Will of Your Father

Forget your desires and pray for what God desires, not for what you desire. This is the primary way to avoid purgatory!

O Jesus, stretched out upon the cross, I implore You, give me the grace of doing faithfully the most holy will of Your Father, in all things, always and everywhere. And when this will of God will seem to me very harsh and difficult to fulfill, it is then I beg You, Jesus, may power and strength flow upon me from Your wounds, and may my lips keep repeating, "Your will be done, O Lord." O Savior of the world, Lover of man's salvation, who in such terrible torment and pain forget Yourself to think only of the salvation of souls, O most compassionate Jesus, grant me the grace to forget myself that I may live totally for souls, helping You in the work of salvation, according to the most holy will of Your Father.... (1265)

God Be Blessed!

Bid me to stay in this convent, I will stay; bid me to undertake the work, I will undertake it; leave me in uncertainty about the work until

I die, be blessed; give me death when, humanly speaking, my life seems particularly necessary, be blessed. Should You take me in my youth, be blessed; should You let me live to a ripe old age, be blessed. Should You give me health and strength, be blessed; should You confine me to a bed of pain for my whole life, be blessed. Should you give only failures and disappointments in life, be blessed. Should You allow my purest intentions to be condemned, be blessed. Should you enlighten my mind, be blessed. Should you leave me in darkness and all kinds of torments, be blessed.

From this moment on, I live in the deepest peace, because the Lord himself is carrying me in the hollow of His hand. He, Lord of unfathomable mercy, knows that I desire Him alone in all things, always and everywhere. (1264)

PART V
Devotions for the Suffering and the Dying: The Promise of God's Mercy

Oh, how much we should pray for the dying! Let us take advantage of mercy while there is still time for mercy. (1035) When I went to the garden one afternoon, my Guardian Angel said to me, "Pray for the dying." (314) Oh, dying souls are in such great need of prayer! O Jesus, inspire souls to pray often for the dying. (1015)

St. Faustina's community prayed this prayer for those who were dying:

O most merciful Jesus, Lover of souls, I beseech You, by the agony of Your most Sacred Heart, and by the sorrows of Your Immaculate Mother, wash clean in Your Blood the sinners of the whole world who are to die this day. Agonizing Heart of Jesus, have mercy on the dying.

St. Faustina knew how important it was to pray for a holy death. And she had a great love for the dying. "God and Souls" was her motto. We're invited to pray with St. Faustina to save souls. We in turn will be remembered at the hour of our death for the graces we need for a holy death, which is to die in the state of grace!

Pray for the dying. A person is dying every second on earth and needs our help. This is their final chance for salvation as they become a holy soul. Mercy on the holy souls will bring us also the crowning mercy of a holy death.

When we pray for the dying we believe God can give that soul the grace for final repentance. We become a "godparent" to that soul and assist them out of purgatory. We have a fresh intercessor for us throughout life.

At the canonization of St. Faustina on the first Mercy Sunday, 1999, St. John Paul II said: "I warmly encourage you to be apostles of Divine Mercy, like [St.] Faustina Kowalska, wherever you live and work."

St. Faustina's Pleas for Sinners

When I immersed myself in prayer and united myself with all the Masses that were being celebrated all over the world at that time, I implored God, for the sake of all these Holy Masses, to have mercy on the world and especially on poor sinners who were dying at that moment. At the same instant, I received an interior answer from God that a thousand souls had received grace through the prayerful mediation I had offered to God. We do not know the number of souls that is ours to save through our prayers and sacrifices; therefore, let us always pray for sinners. (1783)

[Jesus said to St. Faustina:] The loss of each soul plunges Me into mortal sadness. You always console Me when you pray for sinners. The prayer most pleasing to Me is prayer for the conversion of sinners. Know, My daughter, that this prayer is always heard and answered. (1397)

March 15, 1937. Today, I entered into the bitterness of the Passion of the Lord Jesus. I suffered in a purely spiritual way. I learned how horrible sin was. God gave me to know the whole hideousness of sin. I learned in the depths of my soul how horrible sin was, even the smallest sin, and how much it tormented the soul of Jesus. I would rather suffer a thousand hells than commit even the smallest venial sin. (1016)

[Jesus said to St. Faustina:] Pray as much as you can for the dying. By your entreaties obtain for them trust in My mercy, because they have most need of trust, and have it the least. Be assured that the grace of eternal salvation for certain souls in their final moment depends on

your prayer. You know the whole abyss of My mercy, so draw upon it for yourself and especially for poor sinners. Sooner would heaven and earth turn into nothingness than would My mercy not embrace a trusting soul. (1777)

[St. Faustina wrote:] I often communicate with persons who are dying and obtain the divine mercy for them. Oh, how great is the goodness of God, greater than we can understand. There are moments and there are mysteries of the divine mercy over which the heavens are astounded. Let our judgment of souls cease, for God's mercy upon them is extraordinary. (1684)

Jesus, I plead with You for souls that are in most need of prayer. I plead for the dying; be merciful to them. (240)

God's Unfathomable Mercy

O God of fathomless mercy, who allow me to give relief and help to the dying by my unworthy prayer, be blessed as many thousand times as there are stars in the sky and drops of water in all the oceans! Let Your mercy resound throughout the orb of the earth, and let it rise to the foot of Your throne, giving praise to the greatest of Your attributes; that is, Your incomprehensible mercy. O God, this unfathomable mercy enthralls anew all the holy souls and all the spirits of heaven. These pure spirits are immersed in holy amazement as they glorify this inconceivable mercy of God, which in turn arouses even greater admiration in them, and their praise is carried out in a perfect manner. O eternal God, how ardently I desire to glorify this greatest of Your attributes; namely Your unfathomable mercy. I see all my littleness, and cannot compare myself to the heavenly beings who praise the Lord's mercy with holy admiration. But I, too, have found a way to give perfect glory to the incomprehensible mercy of God. (835)

Oh, if only everyone realized how great the Lord's mercy is and how much we all need that mercy, especially at that crucial hour! (811) Have confidence in God, for He is good and inconceivable. His mercy surpasses our understanding. (880)

Divine Mercy Devotion

How precious is your mercy, O God!
>The children of Adam take refuge in the shadow of your wings.
>> — Psalm 36:8 (NABRE)

Our Lord revealed to St. Faustina a powerful prayer He wanted all to say: the Chaplet of Divine Mercy. He promises extraordinary graces to those who recite this prayer. This is one of the best means to assist the dying.

I realize more and more how much every soul needs God's mercy throughout life and particularly at the hour of death. This chaplet mitigates God's anger, as He Himself told me. (1036)

[Jesus said to St. Faustina:] My daughter, encourage souls to say the Chaplet which I have given to you. (1541) Whoever will recite it will receive great mercy at the hour of death. (687) [W]hen they say this chaplet in the presence of the dying, I will stand between My Father and the dying person, not as the just Judge but as the merciful Savior. (1541) Priests will recommend it to sinners as

"Holy water is indeed of great help to the dying." (601)

their last hope of salvation. Even if there were a sinner most hardened, if he were to recite this chaplet only once, he would receive grace from My infinite mercy. I desire to grant unimaginable graces to those souls who trust in My mercy. (687) Through the Chaplet you will obtain everything, if what you ask for is compatible with My will. (1731)

[St. Faustina wrote:] Today, the Lord came to me and said, My daughter, help me to save souls. You will go to a dying sinner, and you will continue to recite the chaplet, and in this way you will obtain for him trust in My mercy, for he is already in despair. (1797)

[Not only will people who say the Chaplet receive these graces, but also the dying at whose side others will recite this prayer. Jesus said to St. Faustina:] When this chaplet is said by the bedside of a dying person, God's anger is placated, unfathomable mercy envelops the soul and the very depths of My tender mercy are moved for the sake of the sorrowful Passion of My Son. (811)

The Chaplet of Divine Mercy

On a different occasion, Jesus said to St. Faustina: "[B]y saying the Chaplet you are bringing humankind closer to Me" (929). And again: "The souls that say this chaplet will be embraced by My mercy during their lifetime and especially at the hour of their death" (754).

- *The chaplet is recited using ordinary rosary beads. Begin with one Our Father, one Hail Mary, and the Apostles' Creed.*
- *On the Our Father beads, pray:* Eternal Father, I offer You the Body and Blood, Soul and Divinity of Your dearly Beloved Son, Our Lord Jesus Christ, in atonement for our sins and those of the whole world.

- *On the Hail Mary beads, pray:* For the sake of His sorrowful Passion, have mercy on us and on the whole world.
- *Conclude with (three times):* Holy God, Holy Mighty One, Holy Immortal One, have mercy on us and on the whole world.
- *Optional closing:* Eternal God, in whom mercy is endless and the treasury of compassion inexhaustible, look kindly upon us and increase Your mercy in us, that in difficult moments we might not despair nor become despondent, but with great confidence submit ourselves to Your holy will, which is Love and Mercy itself. (950)

PRAYING THE CHAPLET FOR THE DYING WHEN NOT PRESENT

Can one who is not present with a dying person obtain mercy for him or her by means of praying the Chaplet of Divine Mercy? St. Faustina wrote the following:

> My contact with the dying is, just as it has been in the past, very close. I often accompany a person who is dying far away, but my greatest joy is when I see the promise of mercy fulfilled in these souls. The Lord is faithful: what He once ordains — He fulfills. (935)

> I prayed today for a soul in agony, who was dying without the Holy Sacraments, although she desired them. But it was already too late. It was a relative of mine, my uncle's wife. She was a soul pleasing to God. There was no distance between us at that moment. (207)

Sacred Thirst of Jesus, save them!

The Way of the Cross for the Holy Souls

"The life of each person, wherever he or she lives, is marked by the cross. Sister Faustina also had a cross; one that was fitting for her. Without it, she would not have been credible; she would not have been a saint," says Sister Elzbieta Siepak, in Ewa K. Czaczkowska's book *Faustina: The Mystic and Her Message.* "Her cross was a very heavy one: she bore the burden of her illness and, in connection with her prophetic mission, a great responsibility for the Church and people's salvation.

"Her struggle with many issues in community life was also a cross for her. Just like a family, a congregation is made up of people with various personalities and various weaknesses, because it is made up of ordinary people, not angels," Sister Siepak emphasizes. She adds:

> Sister Faustina saw the good in her suffering related to life in a community. She saw that suffering purified her of selfishness, of different weaknesses, and created space for love, and as a result transformed itself into a good for herself and others. Her purification made her capable of greater love, a more complete union with Jesus. She was becoming a free person, and as such, she was able to love everyone, even those who were not kind toward her, or who were not good to her. This cannot be achieved by means of the intellect, but only on the way of the cross.

THE WAY OF THE CROSS FREES THE HOLY SOULS

"What salutary insights will the continual meditation on the bitter passion of the Son of God stir up in the soul! Daily experience has taught me that by this devout form of prayer men's lives are quickly changed for the better. For the Way of the Cross is the antidote for vice, the cleansing of unbridled desires, and an effective incentive to virtue and holiness of life. Indeed, if we set the excruciating sufferings of the Son of God portrayed in so many vivid pictures before the eyes of the soul we can hardly refrain from abhorring the defilements of our own life because of the abundant light that fills our souls. Nay, I should rather say that we will be urged to repay such great love with our own love or at least to bear willingly the misfortunes that from time to time in every walk of life fall to our lot."

— St. Leonard of Port Maurice in
Proper Offices of Franciscan Saints, IV, 197

(St. Leonard of Port Maurice, an advocate for the holy souls, promoted the Way of the Cross with such enthusiasm that he was known as the Preacher of the Way of the Cross. He said, "If you deliver one soul from purgatory, you can say with confidence, 'Heaven is mine.'")

The Divine Mercy Stations

Remember, station by station, the passion and death that Christ endured for these souls, for all souls, for your soul.

Pray that the same Christ, the one who conquered death, may soon welcome into the Eternal Banquet the souls of your loved ones, and the souls of all the faithful departed.

Begin each station with:

Eternal Father, I offer you the Body and Blood, Soul and Divinity of Your dearly beloved Son, Our Lord Jesus Christ, in atonement for our sins and those of the whole world. For the sake of His sorrowful passion, have mercy on us and on the whole world.

After each Invocation say: *Have mercy on us and on the whole world.*

Invocations:

1. *For the sake of His Institution of the Eucharist as the memorial of His Passion ...*
2. *For the sake of His agony in the Garden ...*
3. *For the sake of His being scourged and crowned with thorns ...*
4. *For the sake of His being condemned to death ...*
5. *For the sake of His carrying the Cross ...*
6. *For the sake of His falling under the weight of the Cross ...*
7. *For the sake of His meeting His afflicted Mother ...*
8. *For the sake of His accepting help in carrying the Cross ...*
9. *For the sake of His receiving mercy from Veronica ...*
10. *For the sake of His consoling the women ...*
11. *For the sake of His being stripped ...*
12. *For the sake of His being crucified ...*
13. *For the sake of His death on the Cross ...*
14. *For the sake of His being buried ...*
15. *For the sake of his being raised from the dead ...*

Repeat three times: *Holy God, Holy Mighty One, Holy Immortal One, have mercy on us and on the whole world.*

St. Faustina on the Value of Suffering

Suffering is the greatest treasure on earth; it purifies the soul. In suffering we learn who is our true friend. (342) [B]efore we go to our Homeland, we must fulfill the will of God on earth; that is, trials and struggles must run their full course in us. (897)

The holy souls also are in fellowship with those who suffer on earth. The holy souls pray that those who suffer will be spared the pains of purgatory.

HEROIC ACT OF CHARITY

The Heroic Act of Charity was initiated by St. Gertrude (1256-1302). It's a beautiful and effective offering to God, for the souls in purgatory, of all works of satisfaction and suffrages we may gain during life.

St. Gertrude offered all her merits for the dead. She was tempted by the devil at the hour of death. Our Lord reminded her of her heroic act of charity. Not content with sending His angels and the thousands of souls she released to assist her, Our Lord said He would take her straight to heaven and multiply a hundredfold all her merits.

—

O Holy and Adorable Trinity, desiring to cooperate in the deliverance of the souls in purgatory, and to testify to my devotion to the Blessed Virgin Mary, I secede and renounce, in behalf of the holy souls, all the satisfactory value of all my works during life, and all the suffrages which may be given to me after my death, consigning them entirely into the hands of the Blessed Virgin Mary, that she may apply them according to her good pleasure to the souls of the faithful departed, whom she desires to deliver from their sufferings. Deign, O my God, to accept and bless this offering I make to You at this moment. Amen.

They look to those suffering for a tiny share in the merit that earthly sufferings still garner, because they can't gain merit for themselves. Once the soul leaves the body the time of merit is over. Through this sharing, the holy souls can be assisted, while we can improve our final disposition.

O Savior of the world, I unite myself with Your mercy. My Jesus, I join all my sufferings to Yours and deposit them in the treasury of the Church for the benefit of souls. (740)

I see that God never tries us beyond what we are able to suffer. Oh, I fear nothing; if God sends such great suffering to a soul. He upholds it with an even greater grace, although we are not aware of it. One act of trust at such moments gives greater glory to God than whole hours passed in prayer filled with consolations. (78)

Oh who will comprehend Your love and Your unfathomable mercy toward us! (80)

St. Faustina gave thanks to Jesus in all her sufferings:

True love is measured by the thermometer of suffering. Jesus, I thank You for the little daily crosses, for opposition to my endeavors, for the hardships of communal life, for the misinterpretation of my intentions, for humiliations at the hands of others, for the harsh way in which we are treated, for false suspicions, for poor health and loss of strength, for self-denial, for dying to myself, for lack of recognition in everything, for the upsetting of all my plans. (343)

Oh, if only the suffering soul knew how it is loved by God, it would die of joy and excess of happiness! Some day, we will know the value of suffering, but then we will no longer be able to suffer. The present moment is ours. (963)

Patience in adversity gives power to the soul. (607) I see that patience always leads to victory, although not immediately; but victory will become manifest after many years. Patience is linked to meekness. (1514)

Thank You, Jesus, for interior sufferings, for dryness of spirit, for terrors, fears and uncertainties, for the darkness and the deep interior night, for temptations and various ordeals, for torments too difficult to describe, especially for those which no one will understand, for the hour of death with its fierce struggle and all its bitterness. (343)

If the angels were capable of envy, they would envy us for two things: one is the receiving of Holy Communion, and the other is suffering. (1804)

Our Lord told St. Faustina that at three in the afternoon:

[T]ry your best to make the Stations of the Cross in this hour, provided that your duties permit it; and if you are not able to make the Stations of the Cross, then at least step into the chapel for a moment and adore, in the Blessed Sacrament, My Heart, which is full of mercy; and should you be unable to step into the chapel, immerse yourself in prayer there where you happen to be, if only for a very brief instant." (1572)

[St. Faustina was deeply moved by the omnipotence of God's mercy which passed through the heart of Jesus:] In this open wound of the Heart of

Jesus I enclose all poor humans … and those individuals whom I love as often as I make the Way of the Cross. (1309)

Place all those dear to you in the heart of Jesus.

———

Agonizing Heart of Jesus, have mercy on the sick and dying.

The Praises of Divine Mercy

God's love is the flower — Mercy the fruit.

Let the doubting soul read these considerations on Divine Mercy and become trusting.

Divine Mercy, gushing forth from the bosom of the Father, I trust in You.

Divine Mercy, greatest attribute of God, I trust in You.

Divine Mercy, incomprehensible mystery, I trust in You.

Divine Mercy, fount gushing forth from the mystery of the Most Blessed Trinity, I trust in You.

Divine Mercy, unfathomed by any intellect, human or angelic, I trust in You.

Divine Mercy, from which wells forth all life and happiness, I trust in You.

Divine Mercy, better than the heavens, I trust in You.

Divine Mercy, source of miracles and wonders, I trust in You.

Divine Mercy, encompassing the whole universe, I trust in You.

Divine Mercy, descending to earth in the Person of the Incarnate Word, I trust in You.

Divine Mercy, which flowed out from the open wound of the Heart of Jesus, I trust in You.

Divine Mercy, enclosed in the Heart of Jesus for us, and especially for sinners, I trust in You.

Divine Mercy, unfathomed in the institution of the Sacred Host, I trust in You.

Divine Mercy, in the founding of Holy Church, I trust in You.

Divine Mercy, in the Sacrament of Holy Baptism, I trust in You.

Divine Mercy, in our justification through Jesus Christ, I trust in You.

Divine Mercy, accompanying us through our whole life, I trust in You.

Divine Mercy, embracing us especially at the hour of death, I trust in You.

Divine Mercy, endowing us with immortal life, I trust in You.

Divine Mercy, accompanying us every moment of our life, I trust in You.

Divine Mercy, shielding us from the fire of hell, I trust in You.

Divine Mercy, in the conversion of hardened sinners, I trust in You.

Divine Mercy, astonishment for Angels, incomprehensible to Saints, I trust in You.

Divine Mercy, unfathomed in all the mysteries of God, I trust in You.

Divine Mercy, lifting us out of every misery, I trust in You.

Divine Mercy, source of our happiness and joy, I trust in You.

Divine Mercy, in calling us forth from nothingness to existence, I trust in You.

Divine Mercy, embracing all the works of His hands, I trust in You.

Divine Mercy, crown of all God's handiwork, I trust in You.

Divine Mercy, in which we are all immersed, I trust in You.
Divine Mercy, sweet relief for anguished hearts, I trust in You.
Divine Mercy, only hope of despairing souls, I trust in You.
Divine Mercy, repose of hearts, peace amidst fear, I trust in You.
Divine Mercy, delight and ecstasy of holy souls, I trust in You.
Divine Mercy, inspiring hope against all hope, I trust in You. (949)

Eternal God, in whom mercy is endless and the treasury of compassion inexhaustible, look kindly upon us and increase Your mercy in us, that in difficult moments we might not despair nor become despondent, but with great confidence submit ourselves to Your holy will, which is Love and Mercy itself. (950)

O incomprehensible and limitless Mercy Divine,
To extol and adore You worthily, who can?
Supreme attribute of Almighty God,
You are the sweet hope for sinful man.

Into one hymn yourselves unite, stars, earth and sea, and in one accord thankfully and fervently sing of the incomprehensible Divine Mercy. (951)

St. Joseph, Patron of the Dying

St. Joseph was one of the patron saints of St. Faustina's Congregation of Sisters of Our Lady of Mercy.

St. Joseph is the patron of a happy death. Like St. Faustina, we should have a filial devotion to him. His power is dreaded by the devil. His death is the most singularly privileged and happiest death we could imagine, as he died in the presence of Jesus and Mary.

Joseph will obtain for us the same privilege at our passage from this life to eternity. We are called to pray for a happy death (to die in the state of grace) for ourselves, for our families, and for those now near death. It's the greatest and last blessing of God in this life. We must petition God for this grace.

[St. Faustina wrote:] Saint Joseph urged me to have a constant devotion to him. He himself told me to recite three prayers [the Our Father, Hail Mary, and Glory Be] and the *Memorare* ([footnote] 204) once every day. He looked at me with great kindness and gave me to know how much he is supporting this work [of mercy]. He has promised me this special help and protection. I recite the requested prayers every day and feel his special protection. (1203)

Say this prayer daily for the dying: *St. Joseph, foster father of Our Lord, Jesus Christ, true spouse of Mary ever Virgin, pray for us and all those who will die this day or night.*

Memorare to St. Joseph

Remember, O most chaste spouse of the Virgin Mary, that never was it known that anyone who implored your help or sought your intercession was left unaided. Full of confidence in your power, I fly unto you, and beg your protection. Despise not, O Foster Father of the Redeemer, my humble supplication, but in your bounty, hear and answer me. Amen. (1203, 204)

Our Father, Hail Mary, Glory Be.

Psalms of Repentance

The Church and St. Faustina recommend praying these psalms both for the suffering souls in purgatory, the dying, and also in preparation for one's own death.

Psalm 51
A Prayer for the Remission of Sins
Miserere: *"Have mercy"*

Have mercy on me, O God,
> according to thy steadfast love;
> according to thy abundant mercy blot out my transgressions.
Wash me thoroughly from my iniquity,
> and cleanse me from my sin!

For I know my transgressions,
> And my sin is ever before me.
Against thee, thee only, have I sinned,
> and done that which is evil in thy sight,
so that thou art justified in thy sentence
> and blameless in thy judgment.
Behold, I was brought forth in iniquity,
> and in sin did my mother conceive me.

Behold, thou desirest truth in the inward being;
> therefore teach me wisdom in my secret heart.
Purge me with hyssop, and I shall be clean;
> wash me, and I shall be whiter than snow.
Fill me with joy and gladness;
> let the bones which thou hast broken rejoice.

Hide thy face from my sins,
    and blot out all my iniquities.

Create in me a clean heart, O God,
    and put a new and right spirit within me.
Cast me not away from thy presence,
    and take not thy holy Spirit from me.
Restore to me the joy of thy salvation,
    and uphold me with a willing spirit.

Then will I teach transgressors thy ways,
    and sinners will return to thee.
Deliver me from bloodguiltiness, O God,
    thou God of my salvation,
    and my tongue will sing aloud of thy deliverance.

O Lord, open thou my lips,
    and my mouth shall show forth thy praise.
For thou hast no delight in sacrifice;
    were I to give a burnt offering, thou wouldst not be pleased.
The sacrifice acceptable to God is a broken spirit;
    a broken and contrite heart, O God, thou wilt not despise.

Do good to Zion in thy good pleasure;
    rebuild the walls of Jerusalem,
then wilt thou delight in right sacrifices,
    in burnt offerings and whole burnt offerings;
    then bulls will be offered on thy altar.

Psalm 130

A Prayer Imploring God's Mercy
De Profundis: *"From the Depths"*

The Church uses this in the liturgy as her official prayer for the souls in purgatory.
The just, afflicted by their sins, implore the Divine Mercy.

Out of the depths I cry to thee, O LORD!
    Lord, hear my voice!
Let thy ears be attentive
    to the voice of my supplications!

If thou, O LORD, shouldst mark iniquities,
    Lord, who could stand?
But there is forgiveness with thee,
    that thou mayest be feared.

I wait for the LORD, my soul waits,
    and in his word I hope;
my soul waits for the Lord
    more than watchmen for the morning,
    more than watchmen for the morning.

O Israel, hope in the LORD!
    For with the LORD there is steadfast love,
    and with him is plenteous redemption.
And he will redeem Israel
    from all his iniquities.

Be the Safeguard of My Life

O Mary, my sweet Mother,
To You I turn over my soul, my body and my poor heart.
Be the safeguard of my life,
Especially at death's hour in the final fight. (161)

A Plea for Mercy

O Greatly Merciful God, Infinite Goodness, today all mankind calls out from the abyss of its misery to Your mercy — to Your compassion, O God; and it is with its mighty voice of misery that it cries out. Gracious God, do not reject the prayer of this earth's exiles! O Lord, Goodness beyond our understanding, Who are acquainted with our misery through and through, and know that by our own power we cannot ascend to You, we implore You: anticipate us with Your grace and keep on increasing Your mercy in us, that we may faithfully do Your holy will all through our life and at death's hour. Let the omnipotence of Your mercy shield us from the darts of our salvation's enemies, that we may with confidence, as Your children, await Your final coming — that day known to You alone. And we expect to obtain everything promised us by Jesus in spite of all our wretchedness. For Jesus is our Hope: Through His merciful Heart, as through an open gate, we pass through to heaven. (1570)

O Good Jesus

O Good Jesus! O most tender Jesus! O most sweet Jesus! O Jesus, Son of Mary the Virgin, full of mercy and kindness! O sweet Jesus, according to Your great mercy, have pity on me! O most merciful Jesus, I entreat You by Your Precious

Blood, which You poured forth for sinners, to wash away all my iniquities, and to look upon me, poor and unworthy as I am, humbly asking Your pardon, and invoking this Holy Name of Jesus. O Name of Jesus, sweet Name! Name of Jesus, Name of joy! Name of Jesus, Name of strength! No, what does the Name of Jesus mean but Savior? Wherefore, O Jesus, by Your own Holy Name, save me. Suffer me not to be lost — me, whom You created out of nothing. O good Jesus, let not my iniquity destroy what Your almighty goodness made. O sweet Jesus, recognize what is Your own, and wipe away from me what is not of You!

O most kind Jesus, have pity on me in this time of mercy, and don't condemn me in the time of judgment. The dead shall not praise You, Lord Jesus, nor all those who go down into hell. O most loving Jesus! O Jesus, most longed for by Your own! O most gentle Jesus! Jesus, Jesus, let me enter into the number of Your elect. O Jesus, salvation of those who believe in You; Jesus, Son of Mary the Virgin, pour into me grace, wisdom, charity, chastity, and humility that I may be able perfectly to love You, to enjoy You, to serve You, and make my boast in You, together with all those who invoke Your Holy Name. Amen.

Prayers for a Happy Death

Once, when visiting a sick sister who was eighty-four and known for many virtues, I asked her, "Sister, you are surely ready to stand before the Lord, are you not?" She answered, "I have been preparing myself all my life long for this last hour." And then she added, "Old age does not dispense one from combat." (517)

The greatest gift is to die in the state of grace. We must pray for this grace. Practice the Nine First Fridays and Five First Saturdays to obtain the grace of final perseverance for you and your family. (See the Appendix to learn more about these devotions.)

St. Joseph, Protect Us in Death!

O Blessed St. Joseph who breathed forth your last breath in the fond embrace of Jesus and Mary, when death shall close my career, come, holy father with Jesus and Mary, to aid me and obtain for me the only consolation which I ask at that hour — to die under your protection. Living and dying, into your sacred hands, O Jesus, Mary, and Joseph, I commend my soul. Amen.

St. Faustina's Prayers for a Happy Death

O merciful Jesus, stretched on the cross, be mindful of the hour of our death. O most merciful Heart of Jesus, opened with a lance, shelter me at the last moment of my life. O Blood and Water, which gushed forth from the Heart of Jesus as a fount of unfathomable mercy for me at the hour of my death, O dying Jesus, Hostage of mercy, avert the Divine wrath at the hour of my death. (813)

Jesus, hide me in Your mercy and shield me against everything that might terrify my soul. Do not let my trust in Your mercy be disappointed. Shield me with the omnipotence of Your mercy, and judge me leniently as well. (1480)

Mercy Beyond Measure

God, Your days are without end, Your mercies beyond counting. Help us always to remember that life is short and the day of our death is known to You alone. May Your Holy Spirit lead us to live in holiness and justice all our days. Then, after serving You in the fellowship of Your Church, with strong faith, consoling hope, and perfect love for all, may we joyfully come to Your kingdom. We ask this through Christ Our Lord. Amen.

Prayer for the Dying

Eternal Father, by Your love for St. Joseph, whom You chose in preference to all men to represent You on earth, have mercy on us and on the dying.

Our Father, Hail Mary, Glory Be.

Eternal divine Son, by Your love for St. Joseph who was Your faithful guardian on earth, have mercy on us, and on the dying.

Our Father, Hail Mary, Glory Be.

Eternal divine Spirit, by Your love for St. Joseph, who so carefully watched over Mary, Your beloved spouse, have mercy on us and on the dying.

Our Father, Hail Mary, Glory Be.

Holy Aspirations for the Dying

O God, be gracious to me; O God, have mercy on me; O God, forgive me my sins!

O God the Father, have mercy on me;

O Jesus, be gracious to me; O Holy Spirit strengthen me!

O God the Father, do not reject me;

O Jesus, do not abandon me; O God the Holy Spirit, do not forsake me!

O my God, into your hands I commend my spirit; O Jesus, Son of David, have Mercy on me!

O Jesus, I believe in you; O Jesus, I hope in you; O Jesus, I love you!

O Jesus, I place all my trust in Your bitter passion!

O Jesus, I hide myself in Your sacred wounds!

O Jesus, I enclose myself in Your Sacred Heart!

Holy Mary, Mother of God, assist me!

Holy Mary, protect me from the evil spirit!

Holy Mary, turn your eyes of mercy toward me!

O Mary, Mother of Mercy, obtain grace for me from your dear Son!

O Mary, come to my aid in my anguish and need!

O Mary, enclose me in your virginal heart!

O Mary, commend me to your Son; present me to your Son; reconcile me with your Son!

St. Joseph, obtain for me grace and mercy!

St. Joseph, assist me in my struggle!

St. Joseph, to you I entrust my soul. Save it for me!

St. Joseph, remember me, and obtain mercy for me!

O holy guardian angel, do not abandon me, but combat for me and preserve me from the evil one!

My dear patron saint, pray for me!

Jesus, Jesus, Jesus, into Your hands I commend my spirit!

Thank You, Jesus, for Life

Dear Jesus,
Thank You for the gift of life,
and for the blessing to be among those
who know You are the Son of God.

Thank You for the gift of sight that lets me
see the wondrous things You made,
and for my soul to help me see beyond my sight.

Thank You for all things, and especially my heart,
in which You placed magnetic seeds of grace
that draw me forever to Your love.

I know You hold me in the palm of your hand
and shield me with Your Holy Face. Yet, as the years
go by, Lord, I fear the yoke of sickness and pain,
and worry how my life will end.

And so I humbly come to ask you, Lord,
that when my time comes to leave here below,
do not call me by a sudden death,
not by an accident that leaves the mind confused
or the senses impaired.
Not by a malady that wears out the soul,
or at the mercy of evil forces.
Not with a heart filled with hate, or a body racked with pain,
not abandoned, lonely, without love or care,
not by my own hand, in a moment of despair.

Jesus, let death come as a gentle friend,
to linger with me till my earthly bonds are severed.
And may the Blessed Mother, and my beloved saints,
assist me into the joys of heaven,
where You will bid me to remain in Your loving presence forever. Amen.

St. Faustina's Visions of Heaven

Incomprehensible is the happiness in which the soul will be immersed. (592)

God filled my soul with interior light of a deeper knowledge of Him as Supreme Goodness and Supreme Beauty. I came to know how very much God loves me. Eternal love is His love for me. (16)

I do not know how to live without God, but I also feel that God, absolutely self-sufficient though He is, cannot be happy without me…. (1120)

[A]fter Holy Communion, I was carried in spirit before the throne of God. There I saw the heavenly Powers which incessantly praise God. Beyond the throne I saw a brightness inaccessible to creatures, and there only the Incarnate Word enters as Mediator. (85)

Today I was in heaven, in spirit, and I saw its inconceivable beauties and the happiness that awaits us after death. I saw how all creatures give ceaseless praise and glory to God. I saw how great is happiness in God, which spreads to all creatures, making them happy; and then all the glory and praise which springs from this happiness returns to its source; and they enter into the depths of God, contemplating the inner life of God, the Father, the Son, and the Holy Spirit, whom they will never comprehend or fathom.

> "The world will not last for much longer, and God still wants to grant graces to people before its end, so that no one will be able to excuse themselves at the judgment, that one did not know about the goodness of God and did not hear about his mercy."
> — ST. FAUSTINA TO BLESSED FATHER SOPOCKO

This source of happiness is unchanging in its essence, but it is always new, gushing forth happiness for all creatures. Now I understand Saint Paul, who said, "Eye has not seen, nor has ear heard, nor has it entered into the heart of man what God has prepared for those who love Him." (777)

[A] vivid presence of God suddenly swept over me, and I was caught up in spirit before the majesty of God. I saw how the Angels and the Saints of the Lord give glory to God. The glory of God is so great that I dare not try to describe it, because I would not be able to do so, and souls might think that what I have written is all there is…. And all that has come forth from God returns to Him in the same way and gives Him perfect glory. (1604)

—

Jesus, I Trust in You!

PART VI
Frequently Asked Questions About Purgatory

"[I]t is the greatest charity to pray earnestly to God for the freedom of the souls remaining in purgatory, or to assist them by merciful alms as by various other means."

— Marian Founder Blessed Stanislaus Papczyński

Is Purgatory a Place or a State?

In his general audience on August 4, 1999, St. John Paul II stressed that the term "purgatory" does not indicate a place, but rather "a condition of existence" of those who after death, "exist in a state of purification." He said, "Every trace of attachment to evil must be eliminated, every imperfection of the soul corrected. Purification must be complete, and indeed this is precisely what is meant by the Church's teaching on purgatory."

Why Should We Pray for the Holy Souls?

God's justice demands expiation of their sins and places in our hands the means of assisting them. God gives us the power and privilege to release them.

God has bestowed on us the duty, power, and privilege of paying the debts of the holy souls and hastening their union with Him. In return, the holy souls — who welcome the mercy — support us, help us to amend our lives, and to grow in zeal for souls beyond this realm. Their protection will favor us and they will plead for us and present our petitions to the Heavenly Father who loves them.

Where Is Purgatory in the Bible?

Start in the Second Book of Maccabees (12:43-45, RSV; 12:43-46, NABRE), where Judas Maccabeus orders prayers and sacrifices for fallen soldiers who committed idolatry shortly before their death. Their beseeching implies there's hope even beyond the grave for those who defiled themselves.

In the New Testament, St. Paul hints at the cleansing fires of purgatory, "If any man's work is burned up he will suffer loss though he himself will be saved" (1 Cor 3:12-15). He also prays for Onesiphorus in 2 Timothy 1:18. Also, "But nothing unclean shall enter it [heaven]" (Rev 21:27).

What Is the Primary Pain of the Holy Souls in Purgatory?

Their primary pain is the loss of the sight of God. They saw God's face at the particular judgment! The holy souls burn with a "spiritual fever," a yearning for God that surpasses the heat of any earthly fire. Now they long to be with God forever. They cry out, "God, God, I must be with God!" They feel an inexpressible love for God. Now they know how good God is and what joy it is to be with Him. They want to give Him unceasing glory in heaven. St. Faustina experienced this ardent love when she received Holy Communion.

What Are the Most Powerful Means to Assist the Holy Souls in Purgatory?

The Mass is the most powerful means to relieve and release the holy souls in purgatory. Alongside the Mass, the Rosary, Stations of the Cross, Eucharistic Adoration, and the Chaplet of Divine Mercy are most effective to assist the holy souls. (For more information, see a list of published works on page 168.)

Remember to have Masses offered for yourself and others. A living person is still capable of growing in sanctifying grace.

What Are Gregorian Masses?

Gregorian Masses are a series of thirty Holy Masses celebrated on thirty consecutive days for the repose of the soul of a departed person. Gregorian Masses derive their name from Pope St. Gregory the Great, who was the first to popularize this practice. The *Dialogues* of St. Gregory tell of the soul of a departed monk who appeared and declared that he had been delivered from purgatory upon the completion of thirty Masses. The Sacred Congregation of Indulgences declared this hallowed tradition of more than 1,300 years "a pious and reasonable belief of the faithful on the authority of the Roman Curia." Arrange to put these in your will. They're the greatest gift you can give yourself and your beloved dead. (See Resources on page 163 for more information about the Pious Union of St. Joseph for arranging Gregorian Masses.)

Does Offering Thirty Gregorian Masses Always Rescue a Soul from Purgatory?

Although the practice is approved by the Church, there is no official guarantee. Still, it's a custom that both underscores the power of the Holy Mass and reminds us that there are souls in purgatory who need our prayers.

Can the Holy Souls Intercede for Us?

The holy souls are unable to pray for themselves, but they *can* intercede and pray for us while they're in purgatory.

The *Catechism of the Catholic Church* (958) states: "Our prayer for them is capable not only of helping them, but also of making their intercession for us effective." The more we pray for them, the more powerful their intercession is for us!

Why Are the Holy Souls Called "Poor" and "Holy"?

The holy souls in purgatory are called "poor" because their poverty is the loss of the sight of God. Their time of merit is over. They're unable to help themselves and don't know when they'll enter heaven. They're called "holy" because they can no longer sin and they're absolutely sure of their salvation.

How Do We Teach Children About Purgatory?

Parents, grandparents, and others: Help form kind and merciful hearts in children! Teach them about All Souls' Day. Teach them to pray the Eternal Rest prayer for family members and friends who have died. Teach them about purgatory where souls go to be purified. Visit the cemetery where loved ones are buried and pray there for their souls. Suggest ways these little ones can help the souls get to heaven through their sacrifices and prayers.

What About the Souls of Those Who Have Committed Suicide?

The *Catechism of the Catholic Church* (2282-2283) says: "Grave psychological disturbances, anguish, or grave fear of hardship, suffering, or torture can diminish the responsibility of the one committing suicide.

"We should not despair of the eternal salvation of persons who have taken their own lives. By ways known to him alone, God can provide the opportunity for salutary repentance. The Church prays for persons who have taken their own lives."

The best way to move the soul to heaven is to have Masses offered, particularly Gregorian Masses. (See Resources on page 163 for more information about the Pious Union of St. Joseph for arranging Gregorian Masses.)

Why Is Purgatory Rarely Preached?

In the immediate decades after the Second Vatican Council (1962-1965), the topic of purgatory was less frequently taught in religion classes (including in some seminaries) or addressed in homilies because it was deemed "pre-Vatican II" rather than Church doctrine. (In a similar way, Marian devotion was considered antiquated if not nearly obsolete.) A result was a generation of youth learning little or nothing about faith, grace, sin, hell … and purgatory. Later, as teachers or parents, they lacked the knowledge or understanding to talk about purgatory with their own students or children.

Thankfully, there's been a huge turnaround in recent years, and purgatory is one of the most often asked-about topics among the faithful.

Can We Avoid Purgatory?

Yes, yes, yes! We're given the grace to avoid purgatory and must strive to attain heaven because God desires it. God's grace is sufficient to make saints of every single one of us. If we respond to divine grace — not because of our own inherent sanctity but out of humility and trust in God's mercy — we shouldn't have to spend one single second in purgatory.

How Do We Avoid Purgatory?

Do God's will in all things, even the little ones. True love consists of carrying out God's will. Forgive. Attend Mass as often as possible. Apply your indulgences to the holy souls. Read Scripture. Go to monthly confession. The more we resist God's grace on earth, the more prolonged our time in purgatory.

What Are the Spiritual Benefits of Praying for the Holy Souls?

The holy souls have a special commitment to us for two reasons. First, we're helping them enter heaven sooner. We're delivering them from tremendous suffering. And second, what we're helping them attain is the Beatific Vision! The holy souls show their gratitude in proportion to the greatness of their enjoyment.

Because of the holy souls' great love for us, they're concerned about our salvation. Their prayers help us recognize our faults so that we can better understand the malice of sin. Also, they have a tremendous resolve in assisting us to become holy and go directly to heaven. If we submit ourselves to their influence, we can avoid purgatory.

Why Should We Never Stop Praying for the Deceased?

No prayer is ever wasted with God. If deceased persons are prayed for but they have no need of further purification, those prayers are not unavailing. The deceased in heaven receive an increase in their intimacy of God's love and an increase in their own intercessory power as "we are surrounded by so great a cloud of witnesses" (Heb 12:1). St. Thomas Aquinas called this "accidental glory." Always pray for your dead!

Indulgences, Fasting, and Spiritual Warfare

Indulgences

What is an indulgence?

"An indulgence is a remission before God of the temporal punishment due to sins whose guilt has already been forgiven, which the faithful Christian who is duly disposed gains under certain prescribed conditions through the action of the Church which, as the minister of redemption, dispenses and applies with authority the treasury of the satisfactions of Christ and the saints."

"An indulgence is partial or plenary according as it removes either part or all of the temporal punishment due to sin." The faithful can gain indulgences for themselves or apply them to the dead. (CCC 1471)

An indulgence is granted to the Christian faithful who devoutly visit a cemetery and pray, if only silently, for the dead. This indulgence is applicable only to the souls in purgatory. The indulgence is a plenary one, from November 1 through November 8. On other days of the year, it is a partial indulgence.

This indulgence also calls for:

- Reception of sacramental confession.
- Reception of Holy Communion.

- Performance of the prescribed work, such as Stations of the Cross, the Rosary, etc.
- Praying for the pope's intentions — for example, the Our Father, Hail Mary, or any pious prayer.
- That all conditions are met within eight days prior to or after the prescribed work.

What Are Some Other Devotions That Grant Indulgences?

Nine First Fridays: For the practice of the Nine First Fridays devotion, Our Lord promises the grace of final repentance.

Five First Saturdays: For the practice of the Five First Saturdays devotion, Our Lady promises to assist at the hour of death with the graces necessary for salvation.

(At Fátima, the angel taught the children (one of whom would become known as Sister Lucia) the prayers of forgiveness, mercy, and reparation for sin. In 1929, Our Lady again came to Sister Lucia and directed her to establish devotion to her Immaculate Heart through the First Saturdays Devotion. Two years later, in 1931, Our Lord appeared to St. Faustina and offered His Mercy to a world that did not heed the requests of His mother at Fátima.)

Fasting

Benefits of Fasting

- Fasting opens up our hearts to conversion.
- Fasting gives weight to our prayer intentions.
- Fasting strengthens us in resisting temptations.
- Fasting promotes peace in our hearts and peace with one another.

- Fasting teaches us the difference between "wanting" and "needing."
- Fasting reminds us of the plight of the poor and for many in the world who are perpetually hungry.
- Fasting and prayer can free us from addictive behavior.
- Fasting will lead us to a new freedom of our hearts and minds.
- Fasting invites the Holy Spirit to heal our hearts, our relationship with God, and our relationships with others.
- Fasting heals us, the consequences of sin, and the holy souls. Along with attending Mass, praying the Rosary, reading the Bible, and monthly confession, fasting allows us to reach sainthood, attain the fullness of God's love, and defeat Satan.
- Fasting fights against evil that arises within us, our family, our society, and the Church. By giving our bodies, we give ourselves to God, which opens a space for the Holy Spirit to take over.
- Fasting prepares us to work for God and to accomplish His will. We acquire a special spiritual sensitivity and sharpness.
- Humility is a fruit from fasting when coupled with prayer.
- We should fast out of gratitude and encourage others to fast!

In the words of St. Augustine: "Fasting cleanses the soul, raises the mind, subjects one's flesh to the spirit, renders the heart contrite and humble, scatters the clouds of concupiscence, quenches the fire of lust, and kindles the true light of chastity. Enter again into yourself."

A Fasting Prayer

(Adapted from Fast with the Heart, *by Father Slavko Barbarić.)*

Father, today I resolve to fast. I choose to fast because Your prophets fasted, because Your Son, Jesus Christ, fasted, as did His apostles and disciples.

I decide to fast because Your servant, Mother Mary, also fasted. I fast today as a disciple of your Son and I ask for the intercession of the saints and my guardian angel.

Father, I present this day of fasting to You for the ability to discover Your Word more and discover what is essential and non-essential in this life.

I present this fast to You for peace. Peace in my heart, peace within my family, peace with my neighbors, peace in my town/city, state, and my country. I fast for peace in the world, for all troubled spots in the world. I remember those who are hungry and impoverished.

I fast today for (*your intentions*).

Through this fast, cleanse me of all bad habits and calm down my passions and let your virtues increase in me. Let the depth of my soul open to Your grace through this fast, so that it may totally affect and cleanse me.

Father, please help me fast with my heart. Mary, you were free in your heart, bound to nothing except the Father's will. Please obtain by prayer the grace of a joyful fast for me today.

Our Father, Hail Mary, Glory Be.

Spiritual Warfare

Twenty-Five Practical Teachings on Spiritual Warfare Jesus Taught St. Faustina

These teachings from Jesus are a great guide to help you grow in holiness. Our Lord said, "My daughter, I want to teach you about spiritual warfare" (1760).

1. Never trust in yourself, but abandon yourself totally to My will.

2. In desolation, darkness and various doubts, have recourse to Me and to your spiritual director. He will always answer you in My name.

3. Do not bargain with any temptation; lock yourself immediately in My Heart and, at the first opportunity, reveal the temptation to the confessor.

4. Put your self-love in the last place, so that it does not taint your deeds.

5. Bear with yourself with great patience.

6. Do not neglect interior mortifications.

7. Always justify to yourself the opinions of your superiors and of your confessor.

8. Shun murmurs like a plague.

9. Let all act as they like; you are to act as I want you to.

10. Observe the rule faithfully, as you can.

11. If someone causes you trouble, think what good you can do for the person who caused you to suffer.

12. Do not pour out your feelings.

13. Be silent when you are rebuked.

14. Do not ask everyone's opinion, but only the opinion of your confessor; be as frank and simple as a child with him.

15. Do not become discouraged by ingratitude.

16. Do not examine with curiosity the roads down which I lead you.

17. When boredom and discouragement beat against your heart, run away from yourself and hide in My heart.

18. Do not fear struggle; courage itself intimidates temptations, and they dare not attack us.

19. Always fight with the deep conviction that I am with you.
20. Do not be guided by feeling, because it is not always under your control; but all merit lies in the will.
21. Always depend upon your superiors, even in the smallest things.
22. I will not delude you with prospects of peace and consolations; on the contrary, prepare for great battles.
23. Know that you are on a great stage where all heaven and earth are watching you.
24. Fight like a knight, so I can reward you.
25. Do not be unduly fearful, because you are not alone. (1760)

Bibliography and Acknowledgments

Calloway, Donald H., M.I.C. *Purest of All Lilies: The Virgin Mary in the Spirituality of St. Faustina.* Stockbridge, MA: Marian Press, 2008.

Czaczkowska, Ewa K. *Faustina: The Mystic and Her Message.* Stockbridge, MA: Marian Press, 2014.

Dlubak, Nazaria Sister M., O.L.M. *The Spirituality of Saint Faustina.* Kraków, Poland: Misericordia Publications, 2000.

Egan, Harvey D. *Soundings in the Christian Mystical Tradition.* Collegeville, MN: Liturgical Press, 2010.

Kosicki, George W., C.S.B. *Thematic Concordance to the Diary of St. Maria Faustina Kowalska.* Stockbridge, MA: Marian Press, 2015.

——— with David Came. *Faustina, Saint for Our Times: A Personal Look at Her Life, Spirituality, and Legacy.* Stockbridge, MA: Marian Press, 2011.

——— *Mercy Minutes: Daily Gems of St. Faustina to Transform Your Prayer Life.* Stockbridge, MA: Marian Press, 2006.

Kowalska, St. Maria Faustina. *Diary of Saint Maria Faustina Kowalska.* Stockbridge, MA: Marian Press, 1987.

Live the Fast, http://livethefast.org/; P.O. Box 541425, Waltham, MA, 02452; 2014.

Mladinich, Lisa. *True Radiance: Finding Grace in the Second Half of Life.* Cincinnati, OH: Servant Books, 2015.

Siepak, Sister M. Elzbieta, O.L.M. *I Want to Be Transformed into Mercy.* Kraków, Poland: Misericordia Publications, 2008.

Sisters of Our Lady of Mercy. *Litany and Novenas to Saint Faustina*. Kraków, Poland: Misericordia Publications, 2004.

Sister Emmanuel. *Freed and Healed Through Fasting*. Pax Publishing, LLC, USA, 2004.

———

Resources

For information about the National Shrine of the Divine Mercy and to become a Friend of Mercy, go to www.thedivinemercy.org.

Association of Marian Helpers
Eden Hill
Stockbridge, MA 01263
(413) 298-3931

Holy Souls Sodality
c/o Association of Marian Helpers
Eden Hill
Stockbridge, MA 01263
www.prayforsouls.org

For memberships, and to obtain Gregorian Masses, contact:

Pious Union of St. Joseph
953 East Michigan Avenue
Grass Lake, MI 49240
(517) 522-8017
www.pusj.org

About the Cover

A Window into Purgatory
"Purgatory, The Promise of God's Mercy"
28 x 34 inches/Birch Gessoed Panel/24kt Gold Leaf/Acrylic

Icons have been called "windows into heaven" because they let you see inside it. Or, in this case, see inside purgatory. But as with most windows, icons are two-way. As you look in, the ones depicted in the painting are looking out … at you.

When author Susan Tassone asked me to "write" an icon — the verb used for creating an icon — for the cover of this book, the proposal excited me because I've long been interested in, and curious about, purgatory.

As always, before beginning, I researched the intended subject and, more importantly, I prayed. I spent time before the Blessed Sacrament, asking for guidance. I asked Our Lord to guide the hands of His unworthy servant so that I might worthily and perfectly portray His icon. I asked Him to forgive my sins and the sins of those who will venerate the icon. And as she always does, a dear friend sent out e-mails asking others to pray, because icons aren't written on technique alone.

Fundamental to any icon is its symbolism. Symbols play a key role from the very beginning of preparation to the icon's completion. These are the symbols I've included in "Purgatory, The Promise of God's Mercy."

The Panel
The icon is written on a birch panel. The board's vertical dimension is symbolic of the Tree of Life, and its horizontal dimension represents the Tree

of Knowledge. Together they're a reminder of Paradise. A piece of white linen cloth — symbolic of Jesus' shroud — was glued to the board with rabbit-skin glue. Then ten or more coats of white marble gesso (a paint made with marble dust) were applied to it. The white gesso represents the light of creation.

The Image of Christ

- The raised clouds behind Christ are the heavens. They're gold-leafed using 24kt gold. The gold is symbolic of heaven.
- Christ is the focus of the icon. His wounds are present, to help us always remember how He suffered for us.
- Around Christ's head is a halo, the universal symbol of holiness. Inside the halo is the Cross of Salvation, its three arms a Holy Trinity. The Greek letters "ὼ Ό N" mean "I AM WHO I AM" (Ex 3:14).
- Embossed in gold on each side of Christ's head are the letters "IC" and "XC," a widely used four-letter abbreviation of the Greek for Jesus (IHCOYC) Christ (XPICTOC).
- One of Christ's hands blesses us, and the other points to His heart, which holds one of Christ's greatest gifts: His Mercy. His Divine Mercy rays extend to all those in purgatory.

Our Lady Star of the Sea

- In times past, navigators used Polaris, the North Star, to guide them because it holds a fixed position in the sky. Mary, too, guides us, which is why the icon features an embossed star on the top of her head.
- St. Faustina wrote, "I saw Our Lady visiting the souls in Purgatory. The souls call her 'The Star of the Sea.' She brings them refreshment"

(20). This is why, in her left hand, Our Lady is holding a seashell with droplets of water spilling from it.

- Mary's mantle is painted like crashing waves, and on her heart is the Eucharist, with the letters "IHS" (a "Christogram" — a combination of letters that represent the holy name "Jesus"). She is the Mother of the Eucharist.
- Our Lady holds a rosary in her right hand, offering it to an angel who's lifting a soul from purgatory. Those beads, those prayers, are a link, a ladder: soul to angel to Mary to Christ.

St. Faustina

St. Faustina is also shown holding rosary beads. In her *Diary*, she wrote that Jesus said to her: "Say unceasingly the chaplet that I have taught you. Whoever will recite it will receive great mercy at the hour of death" (687).

Purgatory

When I was growing up, purgatory seemed a scary place, with fire and great suffering. It looked like hell to me. After reading Susan's books and having many conversations with their author, I came to a better understanding of what purgatory must be like. St. Faustina described it as "a misty place full of fire in which there was a great crowd of suffering souls" (20).

- The fire is symbolic of their burning love for God, their longing to see His face. So, in the icon, their hearts are painted on fire, with the image of a cross behind them, representing Christ.
- The souls represent various types of people from around the world. They're shown praying not for themselves but for us. Some are pleading for Masses and prayers.

- Three of the souls are painted in white because their time of purification has been completed. They're being pulled out by their guardian angels who are escorting them to heaven.

Most artists sign the front of their work, but I never sign an icon that way. Never. This would be boastful because the icon isn't "mine." Instead, I write on the back in small letters: "Written by the hand of Vivian Imbruglia" and the date.

Somewhere in the icon, hardly visible, are the letters AMDG, which stand for *Ad maiorem Dei gloriam*: "For the greater glory of God." All my work is for His greater glory. This is a belief I live and work by.

My final responsibility is to be the first person to pray with the icon itself. At that point, I cease to see it as my own work of art and view it as the presence of the person or event it reveals.

My job as iconographer is to allow the Holy Spirit to guide my hand and then I stand back and disappear.

Now my prayer is that, while venerating this icon, you'll have the desire to pray for the souls in purgatory.

— Vivian Imbruglia
Iconographer

(**Editor's note:** The icon is permanently located for veneration at St. John Cantius Church, 825 North Carpenter Street, Chicago, IL 60642.)

About the Author

SUSAN TASSONE has long been a passionate champion for the holy souls in purgatory and is recognized as leading a worldwide "purgatory movement."

She's the author of eight best-sellers, including: *Day by Day for the Holy Souls in Purgatory: 365 Reflections*; *The Way of the Cross for the Holy Souls in Purgatory*; *Praying with the Saints for the Holy Souls in Purgatory*; *Prayers, Promises, and Devotions for the Holy Souls in Purgatory*; *The Rosary for the Holy Souls in Purgatory*; and *Thirty-Day Devotions for the Holy Souls in Purgatory*.

Susan continues to work tirelessly to raise donations for Masses for the holy souls, and she is a popular and frequent guest on radio and television shows.

In 2013, she was featured in the groundbreaking documentary, *Purgatory: The Forgotten Church*.

She holds a master's degree in religious education from Loyola University and is a consultant for a major nonprofit philanthropic organization. Susan had the honor and privilege of being granted two private audiences with St. John Paul II, who bestowed a special blessing upon her and her ministry for the holy souls.

Her website is www.susantassone.com.